CARE FOR ME

+ CARE FOR YOU

Take Charge of Your Mental Health while Caregiving

By Alexis Olson, PhD

Edited by Lisa Obermeit, PhD

Care for Me + Care for You: Take Charge of Your Mental Health while Caregiving

Published by Aurora Press

Edited by Lisa Obermeit, PhD

ISBN: 979-8-9920978-0-1

While the information provided is based on research and personal experience, it is not intended as a substitute for professional advice. Readers should consult with appropriate professionals regarding their specific needs.

Printed in the United States of America
First Edition

Table of Contents

Author's Note

The stories in this book are drawn from a blend of clinical and personal experiences. While they are deeply rooted in real-life events, each narrative is an amalgamation of various situations and characters. This approach ensures the protection of confidentiality for all individuals involved. Names, details, and circumstances have been altered to preserve privacy, and any resemblance to specific individuals or events is purely coincidental. My goal is to share the essence of these experiences and bring the interventions to life, offering insight and understanding, while maintaining the utmost respect for the privacy of those whose stories have inspired these pages.

Answering the Call

If you are reading this book, you have likely already been called to caregive, you predict it in the coming years, or you are helping others who have been called to do so. Based on my experience as a neuropsychologist and informal caregiver, the role of informal caregiver often appears by chance—an illness creeps in on a loved one, or a neighbor ages into disability without family nearby to assist. Most who hear the call did not plan their whole lives to be a caregiver. Unfortunately, necessity doesn't wait for us to feel ready or for our depression to disappear; it doesn't call on only those who have ample time and resources, or those who have been a nurturing presence their whole lives. It calls on us as we are, hoping for the best parts of us to answer that call, yet knowing the worst parts may be chiming in like unhelpful backseat drivers.

If this is you, recently hearing the call, it's likely that you are feeling apprehensive, overwhelmed, nervous, self-doubting, or at the very least, curious about what this new role will be like. You may have asked yourself, "Am I capable of this?", "Will I be able to take this on?", or maybe even "Am I the 'type' of person who is the right fit?" Sure, some people are "naturals." As children, they gravitated towards helping others, while the rest of us were resisting the urge to throw that four-square ball at an unsuspecting classmate. If you're among those of us who relate more with the latter, you may wonder if you can rise to the occasion. You likely have self-doubt about whether the state of your mental health or personality fit this role. Fortunately, your personality doesn't need to match Mother Teresa for you to be good at it. In fact, sometimes our more rigid preferences can be harnessed to create even deeper empathy. We can look at another person and think, "I certainly would want X, let me ask if they do too." A deeper understanding of our own human strengths and foibles can help us connect with others.

We won't be radically re-shaping who you "are" with this book. What we can do however, is map out the areas of "You," things like your mental health, personality, and so on. This will help build insight to better understand what parts of caregiving are likely to be easier or harder for you. Then, we can implement approaches that play off of who you are now and help develop parts of yourself that you may need more support in developing.

The tasks taken on at various points in life shape who we are. Many of us become less practiced in caregiving-style tasks. Some personal experiences build the skills necessary for caregiving—e.g., the role of confidant, coach, or class secretary, which each call on and develop caregiving skills, such as empathy, communication, and reliability, respectively. In contrast, other tasks, such as fast-paced, self-directed activities requiring no collaboration or meaningful communication, make us less accustomed to skills called on in caregiving. In turn, these activities can make certain caregiving tasks feel demanding and/or draining. We're simply less practiced in doing them.

I use the term "less *practiced*" intentionally, because most abilities in life simply depend on practice. And practice is something we can choose to engage in. Even if sometimes it is easier said than done. In this book, you'll read about which practices can support you just as you are today. Aspects of psychiatric disorders (e.g., ADHD, OCD), their common friction points with caregiving, and habits and practices that can bring relief are covered. You'll read about the range of emotions, hurdles, and triumphs that caregivers face and how these impact their pre-existing mental health conditions. From anxiety and depression to obsessive-compulsive disorder and other mental health conditions, stories are shared, inspired by those who have navigated this challenging terrain—with names and details altered to maintain privacy. Resources and strategies for proactively (and sometimes retroactively) managing symptoms and caregiving tasks will be offered.

In this book, we identify what practices can support you just as you are *today* and what skills may be helpful for taking care of your loved one tomorrow and beyond. Let's be realistic. The task of caregiving is now—or if you're a planner, it's just around the corner. Regardless of when the call occurs, there is no better time than now to start this journey together.

Who This Book Is For

If you're wondering if this book is a value added to your life, read on. Otherwise, skip to the next section. This book is for those already on or curious about the journey of caregiving while seeking tools to manage the interplay between one's personal characteristics and this role. This book was born out of my clinical experiences as a neuropsychologist working with informal caregivers and their loved ones, as well as my personal experience as an informal caregiver for years. It is designed to resonate with a diverse audience, as each reader brings unique experiences, challenges, and strengths to the caregiving journey. While care needs vary widely depending on the condition, there are many similar experiences that caregivers share. For this reason, the book is geared towards caregiving in general and not towards care for a specific condition (e.g., care for Alzheimer's disease, spinal cord injury, etc.). Many of the ideas within this book largely apply to caregiving for adults, rather than caregiving for children, although some may translate well to caring for either age group. Beyond the type of caregiving, here's who this book is for:

1. **Caregivers on the Path:**

   o   *New Caregivers:* If you are just beginning your caregiving journey, this book offers foundational insights into how your personality traits, mental health, and personal history may influence your caregiving experience. It provides essential guidance for various aspects of your caregiving role.

- *Experienced Caregivers*: For those with more extensive caregiving experience, this book provides an opportunity for self-reflection and further personal growth. It allows you to reevaluate your approach to caregiving and harness your personal characteristics to improve the care you provide.

2. **Those Seeking Self-Understanding**:

- *Personal Growth Enthusiasts*: If you are someone committed to self-improvement and personal development, this book will help you explore how your unique traits can be harnessed for more effective and fulfilling caregiving. It offers a lens through which to understand yourself better.

- *Individuals Navigating Mental Health Challenges*: If you or someone you know is dealing with mental health issues, this book provides a supportive framework to help navigate the complexities of caregiving while managing personal mental health.

3. **Families and Support Networks**:

- *Family Members and Loved Ones*: Family members, friends, or partners of caregivers can gain invaluable insights into the experiences of those providing care. Understanding how a caregiver's personal characteristics and mental health challenges influence their caregiving journey can enhance empathy and support.

- o *Healthcare Professionals*: Professionals, such as nurses, psychologists, and social workers, can benefit from understanding the personal characteristics of the individuals they work within the context of caregiving. This knowledge can help tailor care plans to the unique needs of each patient.

4. **Caregiver Advocates and Educators**:

- o *Advocates*: Individuals, organizations, or professionals advocating for caregivers and seeking to enhance their support systems can use this book as a resource. It equips advocates with a deeper understanding of the multifaceted nature of the individuals involved in caregiving.

- o *Educators and Trainers*: In educational and training settings for caregivers, this book can serve as a valuable tool to help learners comprehend the personal characteristics that influence caregiving, enabling them to provide more comprehensive and effective training.

5. **Those Curious About the Human Experience**:

- o *Curious Minds, Empathetic Souls, & Explorers of the Human Condition*: If you have a fascination for the complexity of the human experience, this book offers an exploration of how personality, mental health, and personal history intertwine with caregiving. It allows you to delve into the dynamics of caregiving through a psychological and personal lens.

How to Use This Book

Welcome to a comprehensive exploration of how your personal characteristics, from personality traits to mental health and personal history, impact your caregiving journey. The structure of the book is "chunked," which is meant to make reading it here and there easy. Just mark where you leave off, then return for the next chunk. Jump to the parts that speak to you and skip others; as caregivers, we often have limited time and need to optimize our efficiency. Here's how to make the most of this book:

1. **Start with Self-Reflection:**

   If you can make the time, begin your journey by taking a moment for self-reflection. Consider your own personality, mental health, and personal history. What are your strengths, challenges, and values? This self-awareness will be a useful reference point throughout the book in helping you identify tools that you can put to good use.

2. **Explore Your Unique Traits:**

   Dive into the sections that align with your specific characteristics and experiences. Whether you're seeking insights into your personality type, managing mental health challenges, or examining your personal history, this book provides dedicated chapters to address each aspect.

3. **Real-Life Inspired Stories**:

   Connect with stories of caregivers who share your characteristics. These case studies offer relatable experiences and insights, showing you how others have navigated similar challenges and harnessed their unique traits for living well while undertaking caregiving.

4. **Practical Tips and Strategies**:

   Discover practical tips and strategies that align with your characteristics. These actionable insights will guide you in your caregiving role, helping you leverage your personal traits for effective and fulfilling care. Many of these are lumped together in the section titled Other Strategies, but others that are deemed central to a specific condition are present in the section for that condition.

5. **Seek Guidance and Support**:

   If you encounter challenges, turn to the sections on seeking guidance and support. Find resources, support networks, and professional advice to help you navigate the complexities of caregiving.

6. **Share and Connect**:

   Encourage open conversations with fellow caregivers, friends, or family members. Share your insights and experiences, and use this book as a conversation starter. It can foster understanding, empathy, and support within your caregiving network.

7. **Review and Reflect**:

   Periodically revisit the book as your caregiving journey unfolds. Your understanding of yourself and your role may evolve over time. Reflect on your experiences and adjust your caregiving approach accordingly.

8. **Customize Your Approach**:

   Use this book as a toolkit to customize your caregiving approach. Tailor your strategies to align with your personal characteristics, and consider the unique needs and preferences of the care recipient.

9. **Share the Wisdom**:

   If you find this book valuable, consider sharing it with fellow caregivers or individuals who may benefit from its insights. Spreading knowledge and understanding can positively impact the caregiving community.

As you embark on your caregiving journey, use this book as your trusted guide, providing you with insights, resources, and tools to make your caregiving experience more informed, compassionate, and personally enriching. The pages within are designed to be your companion, offering wisdom and support for your unique caregiving path.

Caregiving Amidst Mental Health Challenges

There are over 53 million informal caregivers in the U.S., while nearly 1 in 5 individuals in the U.S. experience mental illness (CDC, 2024; SAMHSA, 2023). That chalks up to a lot of people who could be juggling the dual challenge of managing both a mental health condition and the demands of caregiving.

As a caregiver, it's hard to find the time to think about your own needs. Managing one's own mental health condition while caregiving is often not brought up in conversation even with healthcare providers. The experiences of those who face this challenge vary, yet share in being marked by surprise and overwhelm, as well as profound insights into themselves and relationships.

While we won't cover every known disorder in this book, we will cover some common conditions (e.g., ADHD, depression). For each condition covered, we outline core features of the condition, then review caregiving drawbacks and silver linings. We explore how to balance mental health needs and responsibilities—or what to do when that simply isn't possible. Given family caregivers provide an average of nearly 25 hours per week of care—sometimes resources don't allow for all needs to be met. It's a prioritization juggling act. Quite tricky.

About 40 to 70% of caregivers experience subclinical symptoms of a mood disorder. Meaning, even without being diagnosed with a clinical disorder, like major depressive disorder, select symptoms of that disorder are experienced. In the pages to come, you may glimpse yourself in one or more of the conditions discussed. Consider if you (or a loved one) could benefit from the techniques offered, or simply feel better understood.

For those who are both caregivers and individuals managing mental health conditions, the experience can be mind boggling. The following sections tend to the spirit of these caregivers who are working towards providing love, support, and care while simultaneously navigating their own mental health journey.

ADHD: Navigating the Adventure Together

"Life is either a daring adventure or nothing at all."

- Helen Keller

Caregivers with ADHD bring their own brand of spontaneity and creativity to the forefront. ADHD, or attention deficit hyperactivity disorder, is a neurodevelopmental condition characterized by difficulties with attention, hyperactivity, and/or impulsivity. Often thought of as a childhood disorder, many individuals diagnosed with ADHD as children continue to have symptoms of ADHD as adults. Caregiving, a role often filled with responsibility and routine, can present unique challenges for individuals with ADHD. Amidst this whirlwind, caregivers with ADHD bring an irreplaceable and vibrant energy to caregiving. So, fasten your seatbelts for a journey through the world of caregivers with ADHD. Let's take a look at each symptom and how it can relate to caregiving.

Core Symptoms & Impact

Inattention: Difficulty sustaining attention, following through on tasks, or organizing activities.

- Caregivers with ADHD may find it challenging to stick to schedules or complete tasks thoroughly, which can impact caregiving consistency.

- Distractibility and disorganization contribute to difficulty initiating tasks, such that procrastination on important (though often seemingly simple/easy) tasks can increase anxiety in the caregiver and the care recipient.

Hyperactivity: Restlessness, difficulty staying seated, or an inner feeling of being constantly "on the go."

- This constant need for movement and stimulation may affect one's ability to focus on caregiving duties for extended periods, increasing the rate of oversights, particularly on boring tasks.

  Impulsivity: Acting without thinking about consequences, interrupting others, or struggling to take turns.

- Such spontaneous reactions, while often well-meaning in the short-run, can lead to unforeseen challenges or misunderstandings during caregiving tasks (e.g., interruptions/tangents during appointments, skipping important steps when "taking shortcuts," etc.).

Subthreshold Symptoms: Even without a diagnosis of ADHD, you may be thinking, "Wow, this sounds like me!" There are a variety of factors that can influence attention and energy levels. Even the act of caregiving, when sufficiently taxing, can impact attention and lead one to question if their mind is slipping. This stress on one's system can lead to being less vigilant, and cue concerns for a clinical disorder, such as ADHD. It's worth checking into, especially if you already had concerns that you or a loved one might have ADHD prior to caregiving. Without a diagnosis, you can still benefit from the tips and insights in the ensuing pages.

A Caregiving Story: ADHD + Stroke

Amy had always been the spirited, vivacious one in her family. With a heart full of love and a penchant for adventure, she'd seized every moment with enthusiasm. But, as life would have it, circumstances changed when her father, Henry, suffered a stroke.

As a caregiver with ADHD, Amy's life always was filled with somewhat scattered thoughts and ideas. While her creativity was boundless, her ability to organize and manage tasks was a daily struggle. Now, with the added responsibility of caring for her father, these challenges came into sharper focus.

The first hurdle was medication management. Amy often found herself setting reminders on her phone, but more often than not, the alerts were drowned in a sea of notifications. Henry's medication regimen was complex, requiring precise timing and dosages. Missed doses could lead to setbacks in his recovery, something Amy dreaded.

One day, after an emotional visit to Henry's doctor, Amy sat in her car, her thoughts spinning like a top. She felt overwhelmed by the responsibility and her ADHD's relentless nature. "I need to find a way to stay on top of this," she muttered to herself, tapping her fingers on the steering wheel.

Amy decided to reach out to her local support group for caregivers. There, she met Sarah, another caregiver who faced similar challenges. Sarah shared her strategy of using a pill organizer with labeled compartments for each medication, organized by the time of day. Amy thought it was brilliant and immediately ordered one.

The pill organizer proved to be a game-changer. She combined it with a physical checklist and timer, so that notifications wouldn't pile up on her phone and be dismissed. With her newfound organization, Amy ensured that Henry received his medications on time, every time. The stress and anxiety around missed doses lessened, allowing her to breathe a little easier.

However, organizing medications was just one part of the puzzle. Amy struggled with another crucial aspect of caregiving—managing Henry's finances. Bills piled up, and the pressure to ensure they were paid weighed heavily on her. The ADHD-driven procrastination made it challenging to start tasks, especially those involving numbers and paperwork.

One evening, after another late payment reminder from the utility company, Amy decided to confront this challenge head-on. She sat down at her desk with a cup of coffee and

Henry's bills spread out before her. She realized that she needed a structured approach.

Remembering how helpful the checklist was for medication, Amy created a checklist on her computer for bills. She broke down the tasks into smaller, manageable steps. For each bill, she listed due dates, amounts, and a brief description. Then, she set a timer for 20 minutes and started working through the checklist. Although she was drawn at times to shift focus, she reminded herself that it was just 20 minutes, then she could take a break.

With this new method, Amy was surprised to find that the task wasn't as overwhelming as she'd thought. "Pay all the bills" became "make one online payment today," to which she thought, "I can do that!" She also found the timer was perfect for her drive for stimulation–it made her feel like she was in a race against time, which was a little exhilarating and helped her stay on task. She paid the bills systematically, checked them off the list, and stored the receipts in labeled folders. Over time, this routine became more manageable, allowing her to stay on top of their financial obligations.

Throughout this journey, Amy learned to embrace her ADHD as a unique part of her identity. It gave her a creative and spontaneous spirit, a quality that her father had always admired. Although it came with its challenges, she discovered that with the right strategies and support, she could be a dedicated and effective caregiver.

> Meanwhile, Henry appreciated his daughter's unwavering dedication and newfound organizational skills. He noticed her growth and often found himself inspired by her determination. Together, they embarked on a journey of recovery, both in their own ways, each supporting the other in their unique struggles and triumphs.

Task Management

The average caregiver, like Amy in the story above, spends 13 days each month managing tasks (e.g., food preparation, transportation, and dispensing medication). Managing these tasks can be challenging, especially given 70% of adults with ADHD reported having difficulty managing their time effectively. Here are some tailored tips to help you navigate these responsibilities:

1. **Create Routine**: Structure and predictability can be very helpful. Set up a daily routine for caregiving tasks, including medication times, meals, and appointments. This helps in managing time and reduces the risk of forgetting important tasks. Using a calendar or reminders app can be helpful; see the Technology Section of the Versatile Strategies chapter on page 184.

   - Identify daily important tasks

   - Pair tasks together (e.g., medications taken at meal times)

2. **Prime task initiation**: Difficulties with task initiation, planning, and organization can impact creating and sticking to a routine. A couple ways to help are:

   - Incorporate interests into routine tasks to increase engagement (e.g., listen to a podcast or audiobook while doing mundane tasks, like folding laundry; bring nature into the home or step out into nature while exercising with the care recipient).

   - Seek external accountability, like having a friend or family member check in midday to verify certain tasks are complete.

3. **Use Reminders and Alarms**: Utilize alarms, phone reminders, or apps specifically designed for caregiving tasks. They can prompt you at the right times for medication, appointments, and other essential tasks. Set alerts in ways you find most helpful.

   - Consider having a different sound for each type of reminder, such as a chime for medication and a horn for doctor's appointments.

   - If you're often late, set an alert for when it's time to get *ready* for an upcoming appointment/task, which prompts you to get moving so you'll be on time with all the necessary items or people on hand.

   - If reviewing your checklists evades you, consider setting one alert every couple hours that prompts you to review a checklist.

- Set a title for your alarms, like "Mealtime medications," so you're not scratching your head as to why the alarm is going off.

- If you cannot do the task right then, until the task is complete, hit "Snooze" instead of dismissing the alarm.

- If you're feeling bombarded with alerts, consider turning off notifications from other applications. Ultimately, as in the story of Amy, we may need to simplify and move away from smartphone reminders which are often accompanied by a slew of other notifications and easily dismissed without taking action.

- Use other forms of reminders:

  - To help remember items as you leave the house, place a bright post-it at eye-level on the front door with the items written on it.

  - For medication reminders, place the pillbox near the paired task (e.g., next to the water glasses, if you have water with every meal).

4. **Break Down Tasks**: Large tasks can be overwhelming. Break them down into smaller, manageable steps. This makes it easier to start and complete each task without feeling overwhelmed. Let's consider the caregiving task of *preparing a weekly meal plan* for a care recipient. Breaking

this task into smaller steps can make it more manageable and ensure nutritional needs are met efficiently.

- Assess Dietary Needs:
  - Consult with a healthcare provider or dietitian to understand the dietary needs and restrictions of the care recipient (e.g., diabetic, low-sodium, allergy considerations).
  - Take note of the care recipient's likes, dislikes, and any food preferences or aversions.
- Gather Recipes:
  - Collect recipes that align with the dietary needs and preferences of the care recipient.
  - Consider variety and balance in meals (e.g., protein, vegetables, grains).
- Plan the Menu:
  - Create a weekly menu that incorporates the chosen recipes. Ensure it's varied to provide a balanced diet and maintain the interest of the care recipient.
  - Include meals for breakfast, lunch, dinner, and any snacks.
- Create a Shopping List:
  - Based on the menu, compile a shopping list of all needed ingredients.
  - Organize the list by categories (e.g., produce, dairy) to streamline the shopping process.
- Grocery Shopping:
  - Allocate a specific day for grocery shopping. Consider online grocery delivery services if going to the store is challenging.

- o Purchase items from the shopping list, checking for freshness and quality, especially for perishables.
- Meal Preparation:
  - o Designate a day for meal preparation. Prepare and cook meals that can be refrigerated or frozen for easy reheating during the week.
  - o Label meals with contents and date prepared for easy identification.
  - o Store meals in the refrigerator or freezer in properly sealed containers.
- Serving Meals:
  - o Reheat meals as needed; consider writing on the container (on painter's tape) the time it takes to heat to the appropriate temperature.
  - o Present meals in an appealing way to encourage appetite.
- Monitor Feedback and Adjust:
  - o Gather feedback from the care recipient about the meals (taste, portion size, preferences).
  - o Adjust future meal plans based on this feedback to better meet the care recipient's needs and preferences.

By breaking down the meal planning and preparation into these steps, a caregiver can manage this crucial task more effectively, ensuring that the care recipient enjoys a variety of nutritious and appealing meals while also reducing the daily workload and stress associated with mealtime. Ask an AI bot, like ChatGPT, to help you break down a task into actionable steps–you can use the following AI request template: "Break down the task of [fill in task, e.g., choosing an adult diaper] into small, actionable steps that won't be overwhelming."

5. **Create Lists**: Make lists for daily, weekly, and monthly caregiving tasks. Having a visual reminder of what needs to be done can be very effective. Check off tasks as you complete them for a sense of accomplishment. Some task management apps integrate with your calendar (e.g., Google Tasks), which can really be a game changer with getting things done on time. You can even set recurring tasks, so you can see them both on your calendar and in list format.

6. **Prioritize Tasks**: Someone with ADHD recently joked that they have two to-do buckets: Do It Right Now and Do It Later. Not everything needs to be done immediately, but some tasks do. Determine which tasks are urgent and important, and focus on those first. This helps in managing time and energy more effectively. (More in Versatile Strategies section, page 166)

7. **Bulk Prep:** Whenever batch/bulk prepping is possible do it. This could entail sorting two weeks' worth of medication in one setting, or bulk meal prep for the coming week or simply chop and store ingredients. Other areas that bulk prep can happen: refill the next month's worth of medication, buy all frequently used medical supplies (e.g., bandages, sanitizing wipes, gloves), pre-arrange transportation for upcoming appointments, select

the week's outfits (including sox and undies). I'm sure you have a few other tasks that you repeatedly do, that would feel nice to have it already prepped and waiting for you when you need to do the task.

8. **Use Visual Aids**: Color-code medications, use colored charts for schedules, or set up a whiteboard with daily tasks to mark off and erase at the end of the day. Visual aids can be particularly helpful if you're a visual learner or tend to forget verbal instructions.

9. **Set One Important Place**: Keep all important documents, medical records, and caregiving information in one place. Being organized can save a lot of time and reduce anxiety when information is needed quickly.

10. **Take Breaks and Self-Care**: Caregiving is demanding, and it's essential to take regular breaks. Engage in activities that relax you and recharge your energy. Remember, taking care of yourself is vital to be able to take care of someone else effectively.

11. **Focus on the Positive**: Celebrate small successes and recognize the importance of your role as a caregiver. Acknowledging the positive aspects can be uplifting and motivating. (More details in the Versatile Strategies section on page 166.)

Remember, managing caregiving tasks is a significant responsibility, and it's okay to ask for help and use tools and strategies that make your role easier and more effective.

The Emotional Side of Things

Regulating emotions is a challenge for 30-70% of adults with ADHD (NIH 2014), and likely more so when they take on the demanding role of caregiving. Regularly scheduled breaks can prevent burnout and emotional overwhelm. However, having in-the-moment strategies to manage emotional outbursts or regulate emotions is crucial to avoid emotional fallout. Here are targeted strategies that can be applied immediately when you feel overwhelmed or on the verge of an emotional response (circle the ones you plan to try out soon):

1. **Deep Breathing**: As soon as you notice signs of distress, pause and take several deep, slow breaths. Focus on making your exhale longer than your inhale. This can help reduce immediate stress and give you a moment to gather your thoughts.

2. **Counting Technique**: Count slowly to 10 (or higher if needed) before reacting. This brief pause can help you assess the situation more calmly and respond more thoughtfully.

3. **Sensory Engagement**: Engage a different sense to quickly shift your focus. This could be holding a piece of ice, smelling something with a strong scent, or touching a texture. It distracts your mind and helps you regain emotional control.

4. **Mindful Observation**: Choose an object nearby and focus all your attention on it for a minute or two. Notice every detail about it, which can help bring your mind back to the present and away from overwhelming emotions.

5. **Use of Affirmations**: Have a few positive affirmations ready that you can say to yourself in moments of stress. For example, "I can handle this," or "I'm doing my best, and that's enough." This can help shift your mindset from a negative to a more positive outlook.

6. **Step Away Briefly**: If possible, remove yourself from the stressful situation for a few minutes. A short walk or even stepping into another room can provide a break from the emotional intensity, allowing you to collect your thoughts.

7. **Progressive Muscle Relaxation**: Quickly tense and then slowly release each muscle group, starting from your toes and moving up to your head. This helps reduce physical tension that accompanies emotional stress.

8. **Quick Exercise**: Do a brief physical activity, like jumping jacks, a fast walk around the room, or stretching. Physical movement can help dissipate the build-up of emotional energy.

9. **Grounding Techniques**: Use grounding techniques like the "5-4-3-2-1" method, where you identify five things you can see, four you can touch, three you can

hear, two you can smell, and one you can taste. This helps bring your focus back to the present.

10. **Visualization**: Close your eyes and visualize a place that makes you feel calm and happy. Spend a few moments immersing yourself in this place, focusing on the details and how calm it makes you feel.

These strategies can help manage emotions in the moment, providing a way to navigate through intense feelings without becoming overwhelmed. Over time, regularly practicing these techniques can also contribute to better overall emotion regulation.

Managing Emotional Fallout

In the event that the above strategies don't avert an outburst, you may be left managing the emotional hangover of both you and the care recipient (or healthcare provider, etc.). Keep in mind the idea of "rupture and repair" – meaning, conflict is somewhat inevitable, and it's most important to repair the rupture that was created by the outburst rather than attempting to eliminate all conflict (pretty unlikely to happen anyways).

Repairing a relationship after an emotional outburst for a caregiver with ADHD involves empathy, understanding, and effective communication, especially when the outburst is directed towards the care recipient. Keep in mind that even if the care recipient has cognitive impairments that limit their communicative abilities, such individuals still understand emotional expressions and are impacted by them. Here are ideas on how to approach the situation:

1. **Allow Time for Cooling Off:** Both you and the care recipient need some time to calm down after the incident. This ensures that when you revisit the conversation, both parties are more open and less reactive.

2. **Self-Reflection:** Reflect on the triggers that led to the outburst. Understanding these can help in explaining your reaction and in making efforts to manage these triggers more effectively in the future.

3. **Acknowledge and Apologize:** Once emotions have settled, express your regret for the outburst. An apology acknowledges the impact of your actions on the care recipient and shows your commitment to maintaining a respectful caregiving relationship.

4. **Communicate Empathetically:** Explain how you understand the impact your actions may have had on them. Empathy shows that you are considering their feelings and the situation from their perspective.

5. **Provide Context, Not Excuses:** While it's important they understand any underlying factors, like ADHD-related impulsivity, ensure this context doesn't serve as an excuse. It's about providing insight, not justification.

6. **Discuss Future Strategies**: Share the steps you're planning to take to better manage similar situations in the future. This could involve techniques for managing impulsivity, strategies for de-escalation, or seeking professional advice for better emotional regulation.

7. **Invite Their Perspective**: If possible, encourage the care recipient to share their feelings and any suggestions they might have for avoiding similar situations in the future. This collaborative approach can strengthen your relationship.

8. **Demonstrate Change Through Actions**: Actions speak louder than words. Consistently applying the strategies you've discussed to manage your emotions and reactions will help rebuild trust and confidence in your caregiving relationship.

9. **Consider Professional Guidance**: If emotional outbursts are frequent or if navigating the caregiver-care recipient dynamic becomes too challenging, seeking support from a mental health professional can provide strategies tailored to your situation.

10. **Exercise Patience and Self-Compassion**: Repairing and strengthening your relationship is a process that requires time and patience from both sides. Practice self-compassion, recognizing the challenges ADHD brings to caregiving, and appreciate the effort you're making to improve.

Silver Linings

1. **Structure & Schedule:** The structured nature of caregiving can help individuals with ADHD better manage their time and tasks. Even individuals without ADHD often need to become extra organized, structured, and routine about their lives when faced with caregiving responsibilities. Sometimes the urgency and responsibility are just what's needed to spur someone with ADHD into sticking to an organizational system or routine. **The unpredictability of caregiving might initially be challenging, but it can also offer a sense of adventure that aligns with ADHD's love for novelty and excitement.**

2. **Feeling Uniquely Useful:** The energy and creativity individuals with ADHD bring to the task of caregiving can be uniquely appreciated by their care recipient, or those who witness their caregiving techniques. Not everyone has the spontaneous nature that can adapt to the sudden and unexpected tasks that arise with caregiving.

3. **External Support:** Delegating tasks and communicating needs can develop and provide a valuable sense of support and community for caregivers with ADHD. Regular social engagements that they may not have otherwise made for themselves, become more routine when prompted by the task of caregiving.

Depression: Nurturing alongside the Shadows

*"Allow yourself to rest. Your soul speaks to you in the quiet moments,
in between your thoughts."*

- Unknown

As one caregiver with depression put it, "Every. Single. Day. Caregiving gives you all the reasons you need to hate yourself." With a depressive outlook, these "reasons" can be difficult to dismiss. The rate of depression among caregivers is estimated to be between 20% and 40% (National Alliance for Caregiving and AARP, 2015), compared to about 5-17% of non-caregivers who experience depression. In other words, you are not alone if this is you. The data suggests that caregiving is a stress and can be difficult to cope with. Clinically, depression is a mood disorder characterized by persistent feelings of sadness, hopelessness, and a lack of interest or pleasure in activities. For some, it presents more as irritability than sadness. Caregivers living with depression often bring a deep understanding of emotional complexity and the nuances of mental health to their caregiving roles. It's a hidden gift from being thoughtful and self-reflective to a degree that creates angst and misery. Yet, even with the stress and strain, one survey found 83 percent of caregivers report caregiving was a positive experience (NORC, 2014).

Core Symptoms & Impact

Understanding the components of depression can help target solutions to each of their challenges:

Persistent Sadness: *Overwhelming, long-lasting feelings of sadness or emptiness.* E.g., minor mishaps bring a strong sadness, or set-backs seem to erase your definition of a meaningful life.

Lack of Interest: *Diminished interest or pleasure in activities once enjoyed.* Apathy can make it difficult to engage in enjoyable activities or caregiving tasks, especially those that require substantial energy or enthusiasm. E.g., you used to look forward to playing bridge online, but now it just feels pointless.

Hopelessness: *A sense of hopelessness and pessimism about the future.* The sense of hopelessness may lead to feelings of inadequacy or guilt in the caregiving role. E.g., You feel like no matter how you execute a task, there is room for self-criticism.

A Caregiving Story: Shifting Negative Narratives

Anna had known the weight of major depression since her teenage years, an unwelcome companion that had lingered far too long. Despite this constant struggle, she was also the primary caregiver for her younger brother, Ethan, who had been in a wheelchair since a car accident left him with a severe spinal cord injury.

Every day felt like a battle for Anna, not only against her own mental health but also against the mounting responsibilities of caring for Ethan. The heaviness of depression often made it challenging for her to find motivation, and maintaining a positive outlook was a constant struggle. Negative thoughts told her that she wasn't doing enough for her brother, that she was failing him.

One chilly morning, Anna sat on the edge of her bed, her thoughts clouded by despair. "I can't keep going like this," she whispered to herself, tears welling up in her eyes. She knew she needed help, not just for Ethan's sake but for her own as well.

Anna decided to reach out to a therapist who specialized in depression and caregiving. The initial session was daunting, but as she spoke about her lifelong battle with depression, it felt like the weight on her shoulders was a little lighter. In their sessions, she shared the complexities of her role as a caregiver and how her depression magnified the challenges. The therapist worked with Anna to develop strategies to relate to her depression while providing the best care for Ethan.

One of the therapist's suggestions was to engage in mindfulness exercises. While initially skeptical that sitting still could help anything, Anna began to practice mindfulness regularly, learning to observe her depressive thoughts without judgment. This newfound awareness allowed her to disconnect from the reflex of buying into such thoughts, and instead to challenge the negative narratives that often consumed her. A strong one was that feeling tired was a sign of weakness; with her new perspective, she could see that fatigue was a natural part of the process and a cue to give herself a little extra grace that day.

Additionally, Anna joined a support group for caregivers of individuals with physical disabilities. There, she met others who faced similar challenges and emotions. Sharing her experiences and hearing the stories of fellow caregivers provided a sense of camaraderie and validation.

One of the most significant challenges was coordinating Ethan's care needs. His daily routine involved medication management, physical therapy, and regular medical appointments. Anna found it increasingly difficult to stay motivated and organized and ensure that Ethan received the care he needed.

With guidance from her therapist, Anna created a care schedule for Ethan. She started using smartphone apps and reminders to track medications, appointments, and therapy sessions. This newfound structure brought a semblance of order to their lives and relieved some of Anna's anxiety.

Anna still had days when she felt overwhelmed and disconnected from her own emotions. On such days, she leaned on her therapist's advice and her support network, which included friends and the caregiver support group.

A turning point came when Anna's therapist encouraged her to engage in open communication with Ethan about her depressive symptoms. One evening, she mustered the courage to sit down with him and share her struggles. Ethan listened attentively.

"I've always admired your strength, Anna," Ethan said, his voice filled with warmth. "But I worry about you. We're a team, and we can face this together."

Anna's eyes welled up with tears, but this time they were tears of relief. She realized that her distorted thoughts of providing inadequate care were just that—distortions. Ethan's words dispelled much of the self-doubt that had haunted her for so long.

Their open dialogue became a source of strength for both of them. Anna began to include Ethan in the planning of his care needs, allowing him to have a say in his own well-being. This not only lightened Anna's burden but also gave Ethan a sense of agency and control over his life.

As the months passed, Anna and Ethan's bond deepened. They faced the challenges of depression and physical disability together, emerging stronger as a team. Anna learned that caring for herself was a necessity to live fully, as well as provide the best care for her brother.

Their journey wasn't without setbacks, but they faced each day with renewed hope and determination. Anna continued to navigate the ups and downs of depression, knowing that her love for Ethan and newfound open communication were guiding lights in her path. Together, they proved that

> even in the darkest moments, love and resilience could prevail.
>
> In this story, we see that even the trickiest feelings like guilt, vulnerability, and the occasional urge to retreat to a desert island can yield to a bit of support and renewed confidence.

Solutions to Common Pitfalls

Simply knowing respite services are available, even without using them, reduces stress by 70% (Archangels, n.d.). In some cases, simple awareness can buffer the impact of a stressor, but other situations may require more rigorous intervention or proactivity. Circle from the following list of interventions those strategies you want to try next and check them off after you try them out:

- **Consciously Label Fatigue**: The added physical and emotional demands of caregiving can lead to understandable fatigue. But through the lens of depression, this fatigue can be perceived as a guilt-inducing "laziness" or apathy. It's as though you are gaslighting yourself. Just having awareness of this tendency can be helpful in reducing related distress. There is a study that found people who were asked about the weather just before being asked how they were feeling, would report having a better overall mood. The better mood was thought to be caused by their ability to control for the influence of crummy weather on their outlook.

Simply taking note of one's caregiving-related exhaustion can cue relief that it's not depression creeping in again, or it's not that we're a lazy bones–we simply need some rest and relaxation.

- **Counteract Guilt or Inadequacy**: Despite it not being true, depression can make you feel valuable only when you are sacrificing yourself. When you're not sacrificing, you might struggle with feelings of guilt or inadequacy. You might believe you are not doing enough, even when you are doing the best you can. This is such a sticky cognitive distortion. It really *feels* real, even when in fact you're doing the difficult job of caregiving quite well. Other times guilt is more abstract, like feeling guilty about feeling relief that someone took over caregiving duties or a loved one passed and you no longer need to care for them. Check out the sections noted below for good counterarguments to those heavy feelings:

  o Celebrating Small Successes (page 169)

  o Inner Critic (page 35).

  o Guilt when Delegating Tasks (page 43)

- **Set Social Minimums**: Have most of your previous social connections gone silent? Caregivers often experience social isolation. They isolate themselves due to the time commitment of caregiving combined with depression making social interactions appear more laborious. It can happen insidiously, which is why monitoring for a baseline amount of social activity is useful. Setting a minimum for oneself, like "I will call a friend twice per week," helps.

- **Advocate for Social Connection**: Sometimes social isolation occurs because friends or family gradually visit less by happenstance or out of avoidance of a situation that seems unrelatable (e.g., they don't know what to say). That social distance creates a space that depression fills with thoughts of self-blame and/or feelings of worthlessness. Not super helpful. Especially since typically they don't have something against you personally, it's instead a matter of a busy schedule and lack of imagination. Consider educating them (I know, one more thing on your plate…) on what type of connection is helpful for you (e.g., say or send a message like, "A quick hello from you or hearing a funny story from your life really brightens my day. It can get pretty isolated over here. I look forward to your messages, even brief ones." (Feel free to cut and paste that and send it to a friend.)

- **Anticipate unsettling milestones:** Some moments in caregiving may affect the caregiver with depression more poignantly, such as witnessing deterioration in a care recipient's condition (e.g., loss of a certain ability level).

  - Be as informed as possible about the known milestones for your loved one's condition. Consider making a list of closely anticipated changes. It's natural to have some level of denial; often we block out indicators of decline so we don't feel the immediate emotional impact. This works in the short term, but can lead to a level of shock when a typical yet unanticipated change occurs.

- o Solicit from other caregivers how they have managed these changes so you feel more prepared. (Caregiver support groups locally or online, like Reddit.com, can be very helpful for this.)

- o Set a regular time to reflect on observed changes in your loved one's abilities (e.g., monthly or quarterly; *not* daily, we're not trying to ruminate on it, just check in periodically). Sometimes a change in ability seems "out of the blue" and more disturbing than if the onset were processed in a more gradual way.

- **Self-Health Check-ins**: Individuals may neglect their own health needs, both physical and mental, as they focus on the needs of the person they are caring for. Having depression makes one more likely to face motivational issues that can lead to neglect of health needs. Here are some strategies that might help:

- o Take a written account of your health needs, review it regularly and see if anything needs more attention.

- o Setting one day a week or month to check in can be helpful.

- o Write an email to yourself with a list of health needs to check in on (e.g., routine bloodwork, dental checkup, etc.), hit send, then hit snooze after reviewing the list and arranging for your health needs.

- ○ Consider having an accountabili-buddy–a supportive person who can check in with you or who you review your list of health needs with to enhance motivation and provide encouragement.

- **Investigate Irritability**: Have you been rude to a loved one or hurried along an unpleasant task? These are signs of irritability. The combination of stress from caregiving and the irritability often associated with depression can lead to increased frustration or anger, sometimes (unintentionally) directed at the person being cared for. No need to pile on the guilt (it's in good supply already!). If you notice anger or irritability has cropped up, see if you can identify the root cause of it. Usually there's a key contributor to the moment's outburst or irritation. Here are a few questions to ask yourself about common contributors to feeling irritated:

  - ○ Am I overwhelmed by something specific? Do I need to simplify something or seek support? (See the section on Prioritizing Tasks or Task Management in the Versatile Strategies section on page 166.)

  - ○ Am I in grief? Grief from a decline in a loved one's condition or anticipated decline? Grief from a loss of freedom due to caregiving responsibilities? Consider seeking the support of a loved one or therapist to help organize and process these feelings.

- Am I expecting something from the care recipient that they can't give? Like more gratitude (which they can't signal very well or simply are unlikely to give)? Naming it for what it is can help. So can finding alternative ways to meet that expectation, like finding outside sources of validation or identifying nonverbal cues that show you they are benefiting from your care (e.g., improved posture, relaxed body language).

- **Optimize Decision Making**: Depression can impair concentration and decision-making abilities, which can become particularly problematic when these skills are needed for effective life management and caregiving. To safeguard against its impact:

  - Defer important decisions (e.g., selecting a healthcare plan) until your depressive episode has lifted a bit or after a good night's sleep.

  - Defer decisions until your caregiving burden is lighter. (Keep in mind, caregiving itself can also impact attentiveness; if you find you are making mistakes or oversights *and* you have a heavy caregiving burden, you'll want to address the caregiving burden as well as the depression symptoms.)

- **Keep a Pulse on Emotions**: To cope with overwhelming emotions, some may become emotionally numb or detached from the rich emotional experiences of life, impacting their ability to provide empathetic care. People who are emotionally detached might struggle to experience or express emotions, even in situations that would normally elicit a strong emotional response. For example, at social gatherings you might smile and engage in conversations mechanically without genuine interest or emotional involvement. Over time, you may avoid situations that require emotional investment, such as dating or deep conversations with friends, preferring to stay in a state of emotional neutrality where you feel more in control and less vulnerable. Overcoming it involves a multifaceted approach, including therapy, mindfulness practices, and developing a better understanding about emotions, which we refer to as "emotional literacy." If you find you relate to any of this, try some of the following techniques:

- Learn to identify and name emotions: This can help in understanding and expressing feelings more effectively. Learning this also helps us to catch emotions early on, eventually catching them before we react in regretful ways. There are tools and resources available to enhance emotional literacy, such as a feelings wheel (found at feelingswheel.com or other sites), body scan meditations (doctorolson.com/media), or other online resources and apps. The goal is to amp up your ability to recognize, label, and hold space for a variety of emotions in their nuanced forms.

- Let the emotional juices flow: Engage in creative outlets (e.g., writing a poem, dancing to a favorite song, or even creating a new recipe) or reflect on past experiences (e.g., reminisce about an emotionally charged memory), gradually building emotional connections. It will likely feel ridiculous at times–after all, most of us are not trained artists or modern dancers (feel free to dance alone with the lights out, just watch out for furniture). Even so, this practice can facilitate reconnecting with emotions and improve overall emotional health.

- **Gratitude Boosts**: A particularly well-researched and helpful intervention is taking a moment to reflect on a few things that you are thankful for. You could do this at a certain time of day, or whenever you feel a boost would be helpful. In fact, doing such exercises regularly can lead to lower stress hormone levels and improved relationship satisfaction (Algoe, Gable, & Maisel, 2010; Lambert et al., 2012).

- **Monitor Care Quality**: The combination of depressive symptoms and the demands of caregiving can sometimes lead to compromised quality of care, as the caregiver struggles to continue managing care among competing emotional demands.

  - <u>Take an honest look</u>: It can be hard to take an honest look and see the ways in which one is falling short. It can feel like a self-fulfilling prophecy: "I already felt guilty and inadequate, this just proves me right!" Juggling depressive symptoms and caregiving is a beast... two beasts! So go easy there, but do be honest. If you see areas that need more diligent care, write them down, make a plan, and solicit support as needed. See the Versatile Strategies section (page 166) for tips on prioritizing, including a questionnaire designed to gauge care alignment with the values and preferences of the care recipient.

- o <u>Use a Lifeline</u>: If a high priority item isn't getting done, consider reaching out to a caregiver support network in your area or the care recipient's healthcare provider, and asking what they suggest. The last thing you want to do is waste your emotional energy beating yourself up, when that same energy can bring you to a good solution.

Harness Emotional Energy

As briefly stated in the prior sentence, the same energy used to beat yourself up over small or big oversights can be used to bring you good solutions and motivate follow-through. My dad would say, "Your psyche will get you to where you're going, but you're responsible for what shape you're in when you get there." I think he meant that instead of squandering energy, it's more helpful (and more enjoyable) to shift your focus to the outcome, learn what you can along the way, and move forward. Remind yourself "there will always be an outcome," e.g., you're going to remember or forget the dose of medication. You can stress yourself out *along the way to* that outcome and arrive beaten down, or you can harness those emotional cues and arrive at that *same* outcome with lessons learned and emotional energy in your tank.

That Pesky Inner Critic

Silencing an inner critic that persistently suggests you're never doing enough (or some other unhelpful commentary) is a common challenge for caregivers, and even more common for those dealing with depression. An inner critic refers to the internal voice that critiques, judges, or demeans a person's actions, thoughts, or feelings. It's a mental dialogue that often focuses on negatives, magnifies faults, and undermines self-confidence. It often occurs automatically, and sometimes without our conscious awareness, constantly narrating our lives in the background and speaking judgments about what we are doing and how well we are doing it. For example, we may say things to ourselves like, "I'm not doing enough," "I should have…," "ugh, I always do this, I always forget to give them their medication on time," or "I'm so bad at this."

This critical inner voice can stem from various sources, including past experiences, societal expectations, upbringing, and personal beliefs. It can really zap one's motivation and happiness, and cause other issues as well, such as:

1. **Reduced Self-Esteem and Confidence**: Persistent self-criticism can erode self-esteem and confidence. It can lead to feelings of worthlessness or inadequacy, making it challenging to appreciate one's own value and accomplishments.

2. **Increased Anxiety and Stress**: The inner critic can heighten feelings of anxiety and stress, especially in

situations where individuals feel they must meet high standards or face potential judgment from others.

3. **Impaired Decision-Making**: Constant self-doubt can hinder decision-making abilities. Individuals may struggle to trust their own judgment, leading to difficulties making decisions or reliance on others for validation.

4. **Interpersonal Problems**: An overly critical inner voice can affect relationships. It may lead to projecting insecurities onto others, difficulty in accepting constructive criticism, or withdrawal from social interactions.

5. **Hindered Personal Growth**: The inner critic can prevent individuals from trying new things or taking risks due to fear of failure or not living up to self-imposed standards.

6. **Perfectionism**: The inner critic often drives perfectionism, leading to unrealistic expectations and an inability to be satisfied with one's efforts and achievements.

7. **Procrastination and Avoidance**: To avoid the discomfort of self-criticism, individuals may procrastinate or avoid tasks and opportunities, limiting personal and professional growth.

8. **Physical Health Issues**: Chronic stress caused by a harsh inner critic can lead to physical health issues,

including sleep disturbances, digestive problems, and a weakened immune system.

Quieting the inner critic involves awareness, challenging negative thoughts, and practicing self-compassion. Techniques like mindfulness, cognitive-behavioral strategies, and seeking support from therapy can be effective in mitigating the impact of the inner critic. Remember, the inner critic is driven by a desire to provide the best possible care, but needs to be balanced with a realistic understanding of what is achievable and a healthy dose of self-compassion.

Engaging in a dialogue with your inner critic is a therapeutic technique that involves acknowledging and responding to your critical inner voice in a constructive way. This process can help you understand and manage the negative thoughts that often contribute to feelings of inadequacy or self-doubt.

Here's how you can have a dialogue with your inner critic:

1. **Identify the Inner Critic's Voice:**

   a. First, recognize when your inner critic is speaking. These are often the thoughts that critique or judge you harshly. For example, you may find yourself saying things like "I'm not smart/talented/strong enough" or "How could I be so stupid?"

   b. Notice the tone and words used by your inner critic. Are they harsh, demeaning, or unrealistic? Is it a familiar voice of a person in your life/past? Were these things you heard from your parents growing up, a boss who was hard on you, a relationship that was not emotionally supportive?

2. **Acknowledge the Critic's Presence**: Instead of trying to silence or ignore the critic, acknowledge its presence. For example, say to yourself, "I hear you, but I may not agree with you."

3. **Understand the Critic's Intent**: Often, the inner critic is trying to protect you from failure or hurt in a misguided way. Ask yourself, "What is the critic trying to protect me from?" (Granted, there is a better solution to this than engaging in berating inner-commentary.)

4. **Respond with Compassion**: Address your inner critic as you would a friend. Offer understanding and compassion. For instance, "I understand you're worried about me failing, but it's okay to make mistakes."

5. **Challenge the Critic's Statements**: Question the validity of the critic's statements. Are they based on facts or are they based on assumptions? For example, "Is it really true that I <u>always</u> fail, or have there been times when I've succeeded?"

6. **Reframe Negative Thoughts**: Replace the critic's harsh words with more positive, realistic statements. Turn "You're not good enough" into "I am doing my best, and that's enough" or "that's what we're working with right now."

7. **Affirm Your Qualities and Strengths**: Remind yourself of your strengths, past successes, and positive qualities. This can help counterbalance the critic's negativity. Can you imagine how life would be different if you reminded yourself of your successes as much as you remind yourself of your imperfections?

8. **Seek a Balanced Perspective**: Aim for a balanced view of the situation. Acknowledge your flaws while also recognizing your capabilities and worth.

9. **Practice Mindfulness**: Mindfulness can help you observe your thoughts without getting caught up in them. It allows you to detach from the inner critic and view its comments more objectively.

10. **Visualize a Supportive Figure**: Imagine a supportive figure (a mentor, friend, or even a version of yourself) who offers encouragement and constructive feedback.

11. **Regular Reflection**: Dedicate time regularly to reflect on your thoughts and the dialogue with your inner critic. Journaling can be an effective tool for this.

12. **Professional Support**: If the inner critic is particularly overwhelming, consider seeking help from a therapist. They can provide strategies to manage and transform these internal dialogues.

Engaging in this kind of dialogue with your inner critic allows you to understand and manage self-critical thoughts better, leading to improved self-esteem and emotional well-being. Remember, it's a practice that takes time and patience.

Below are some common critiques launched by that pesky inner critic and strategies to manage such critical thoughts—check off the responses to your inner critic as you try them out:

1. **"You're not doing enough."**

   - New response: "I am doing the best I can with the resources and time I have. Caregiving is not about doing everything; it's about doing what's necessary." Acknowledge that caregiving has its limits, that you are only human and there is only so much time in the day.

2. **"You should be able to handle this better."**

   - New response: Counter with, "Caregiving is challenging, and it's normal to feel overwhelmed. It is perfectly normal to struggle at times and/or feel anxious or overwhelmed."

3. **"You shouldn't need a break; you're being selfish."**

   - New response: Reinforce the need for self-care by saying, "Taking breaks is essential for my well-being and makes me a better caregiver. It's not selfish to look after my health. If I think it is important for my loved one to be cared for, shouldn't it also be important for me to be cared for?"

4. **"Others would do this job better than you."**

    - New response: Remind yourself of your unique qualities by saying something like, "Every caregiver brings their own strengths and weaknesses. I am doing my best and continuously learning." You can also remind yourself that when you are observing other caregivers, you may only be seeing the good moments while behind the scenes they are struggling just as much as you. A way of doing this is by attending caregiver support groups, where caregivers often feel comfortable sharing their struggles more openly.

5. **"If you really cared, you wouldn't feel frustrated or angry."**

    - New response: Validate your feelings, "It's natural to feel a range of emotions in caregiving. Feeling frustrated doesn't mean I care any less. If I truly didn't care, I wouldn't be bothered at all, ever, which just isn't realistic. Or it would mean I wouldn't take any action, because I wouldn't care!", "frustration and anger are normal feelings that everyone experiences from time to time."

6. **"You made a mistake; you're not cut out for this."**

    - New response: Recognize that mistakes are part of the learning process, "Making a mistake doesn't define my entire caregiving journey. It's an opportunity to learn and improve."

7. **"You should always be available for the person you're caring for."**

   - New response: Set realistic boundaries, "Being available is important, but I also need time for myself. Balancing caregiving with personal time makes me more successful and joyful in both spheres."

8. **"You shouldn't ask for help; you should be able to do this on your own."**

   - New response: Emphasize the value of support, "Seeking help is a sign of strength, not weakness. It's okay to rely on others. We're stronger together." Or, "If it is okay for my loved one to need help, then it makes sense it would be okay for me to need help too."

In combating these critical inner voices, it's important for caregivers to practice self-compassion and recognize the challenges of their role. Regularly engaging in positive self-talk and seeking support from others can help mitigate these negative thoughts and foster a more realistic and kind perspective towards oneself. It is helpful to think objectively about each situation. If that is hard to do, another technique is to try taking the perspective of what one would say to a friend if they were in the same position. If all else fails and your inner critic refuses to take a day off, you might as well start charging it rent for living in your head. At least then, you can save up for something nice – like a vacation from overthinking!

Guilt When Delegating Tasks

For caregivers who experience depression (and many who do not), delegating caregiving tasks can bring an extra serving of guilt. This guilt may stem from an internal narrative that equates delegating with failure or inadequacy in their caregiving performance. It's crucial to address and manage these feelings to maintain both your mental health and the quality of care you provide. Let's break them down and look at possible solutions.

Understanding the Source of Guilt:

Even though we know guilt adds a level of unneeded suffering to the caregiving, it can be hard to shake the feeling. Depression can skew self-perception, leading to undue self-criticism and a heightened sense of responsibility. When you delegate tasks, do you feel like you are not doing enough or are letting down your loved one? If so, keep in mind, one of the symptoms of depression can be guilt. Meaning, when you feel this way, it may not reflect the reality of the situation, but rather it's the depression or the "inner critic" talking (see section above).

Try out and check off these strategies for managing guilt:

- **Rationalize Your Decision to Delegate**: Understand that caregiving is a demanding job, and no one person can handle it all alone. Delegating is not a sign of weakness but a strategic move to ensure comprehensive care for your loved one. A business owner could not run a successful business without hiring others to carry out many of the necessary tasks. You are no different. Try thinking of yourself as the CEO of your caregiving domain. Delegating will overall make this run more efficiently.

- **Openly Communicate with the Care Recipient**: When possible, have a conversation with the person you're caring for, explaining why delegating certain tasks is necessary. Often, they will understand and support your decision, which can help alleviate feelings of guilt.

- **Acknowledge Your Limits**: Knowing your limits is like using GPS. It's there to tell you when to stop and ask for directions before you end up hitting a wall. Recognize and accept your physical and emotional limits. Remember, taking on more than you can handle is not beneficial for either you or the care recipient. For example, while assisting your loved one with getting dressed, you might suddenly feel a wave of frustration, realizing you're becoming short-tempered. This moment of clarity shows you've reached an emotional limit.

- **Focus on Quality, Not Quantity**: Understand that by delegating, you can focus better on the tasks you continue to handle, thus improving the overall quality of care.

- **Ask Yourself if Your Inner Critic is the Cause:** Perhaps one of the critiques leveled by your inner critic is bringing you down when delegating. (See previous section for details.)

Dealing with a Downer (Care Recipient)

If you've experienced it, you know that caring for someone who's always finding the cloud in every silver lining can be such a schlep, especially when you also experience depression symptoms. Empathizing and seeking to understand the root of their complaints seems to go nowhere fast. Even after some gentle nudging, they can continue with their negativity. The below strategies may help in limiting the intensity or impact of their discontentedness:

- **Communicate limits gently but firmly**: It's important to let them know what kind of behavior is acceptable. For example, you can say, "I want to help you, but when you yell, it makes it hard for me to listen. Speak softer."

- **Encourage positive interactions**: Let them know when their interactions are positive and enjoyable for you, reinforcing the behavior you want to see. It may feel Pollyanna-ish but, trust me, it can be surprising how often it works. Here are a few ways to do that:

    - <u>Acknowledge and Amplify</u>: "I'm so glad you enjoyed the chicken soup; I made it thinking of how cozy it feels on a rainy day like this. It warms my heart to see you savoring it."

- ○ <u>Connect on a Personal Level</u>: Share a brief personal sentiment or story related to what they appreciated, fostering a connection. "You know, sunny days like this always remind me of our family picnics. It's lovely, isn't it?"

- ○ <u>Encourage Sharing</u>: Prompt them to express more of what they enjoy. "Is there anything else that's been making your days a bit brighter? I love hearing about it." Consider planting a seed for future positive comments by setting a time for regular reflection, like saying, "It would be nice to hear more about what you enjoy, tell me more at lunch tomorrow" (or some similar regular interval).

- ○ <u>Gratitude for Gratitude</u>: "Thank you for noticing and saying 'thank you'. It means a lot to me that you appreciate the little things." Or, "I love doing these little things for you, especially when I see how much you appreciate them."

- **Redirect conversations**: Gently steer conversations towards more positive or neutral topics when possible. If that doesn't work, simply say, "Let's shift focus" and start talking about a more positive topic, like, "...I heard the Rolling Stones are performing nearby. They sure can rock." You may wish to include a reason why shifting focus (e.g., say, "this is too negative for me today") or not, either is completely fine.

- **Ask a question:** Sometimes when people are critical without providing much direction, placing the action back in their hands can help. For example, if someone is complaining, ask them, "what would you like to do about it" or "how would you like me to help?" This gives them ownership over the problem instead of simply providing criticism of others' decisions.

- **Realize the limits of your influence:** You can provide support and try to create a positive environment, but you cannot change someone's personality or attitude. Pivot your focus towards what you can control. You can start by trying a mindfulness or gratitude exercise (see page 97), or even turn on some music and tune out the negative comments.

Silver Linings

Just like the person we described above, it's easy for us to get caught up in our day-to-day grind and start focusing on the clouds, especially when depression is present. It can be helpful for caregivers to focus on the silver linings from time to time. In fact, scientists have found that one of the biggest predictors of happiness is actually the practice of gratitude (Witvliet et al., 2019), so let's learn about some of the ways in which caregiving offers a silver lining. For example:

1. **Enhanced Sense of Purpose and Self-Worth:** Caregiving can provide a strong sense of purpose and fulfillment, helping to counter feelings of worthlessness or hopelessness often associated with depression. In fact, a

strong sense of purpose serves as a protective factor against depression, even amidst significant life stressors (Boreham & Schutte, 2023).

2. **Structured Routine**: The routine and structure required in caregiving can be beneficial for individuals with depression, providing a sense of stability and normalcy. Familiar routines act as an emotional anchor, resulting in more resilience to stress (Ecker et al., 2023). Routine can help alleviate the sense of helplessness or overwhelm that often accompanies depression.

3. **Increased Social Interaction**: Caregiving often involves interaction with others (e.g., care recipient, in-home health aides, etc.), which can help reduce the isolation and loneliness that frequently accompany depression. The number one contributor to happiness at the end of life was having a close relationship with another person (John Templeton Foundation, April 9, 2024). Through caregiving, not only are you providing this for yourself, you are also providing this for the person you are caring for.

4. **Emotional Rewards**: The emotional connection that can develop through caregiving can be deeply rewarding and uplifting. Altruistic acts, such as caregiving, are protective against depressive episodes (Miller et al., 2021). On top of that, receiving gratitude and appreciation from those being cared for can boost self-esteem and counteract hopelessness. This acknowledgement for a job well done has been found to result in fewer depression symptoms

(Kranabetter & Niessen, 2019). In the opposite direction, caregivers who keep a journal of "good things," gratitude for/acknowledgement of three positive daily experiences, enhance their wellbeing (Kurinobu et al., 2024).

—

As we reflect on the strategies and insights shared in this chapter, one key takeaway is recognizing that a new relationship with depressive symptoms can be formed, one with a sense of choice over where we hold our attention, even if we can't eliminate the Inner Critic entirely. Of further importance is knowing that you are not alone in this experience, and the act of leaning on those in our network does not have to be guilt-ridden. Depression, while daunting, can be managed with the right tools, resources, and support systems. Whether it's through therapy, support groups, medication, or simply opening up to friends and family, finding avenues to express and address your feelings is crucial.

Moreover, the act of caregiving, even in the throes of depression, is a testament to the strength and compassion inherent in each caregiver. While acknowledging the difficulties, we can also recognize the moments of joy, the small victories, and the deep sense of purpose that caregiving can provide.

Remember, your mental health is just as important as the care you provide. Taking steps to care for your emotional and psychological well-being is not a sign of weakness, but a courageous act of self-love and a critical component of effective caregiving.

Anxiety: Riding the Waves of Caregiving

"You don't have to control your thoughts; you just have to

stop letting them control you."

- Dan Millman

Caregivers facing anxiety bring an attentiveness par non, but one which can wear them out. Caregiving with anxiety is a space where concern can be stretched thin or overcharged, but also where being open about your vulnerabilities can lead to balance and well-being. We'll explore ways of breaking the cycle of anxious thinking. Even in chaotic moments, caregivers with anxiety can develop the ability to find those moments of peace and connection.

Core Symptoms of Anxiety

Excessive Worry: Persistent, distressing thoughts about various concerns.

Physical Symptoms: Symptoms like restlessness, muscle tension, and rapid heartbeat.

Avoidance Behaviors: Avoiding situations that trigger anxiety or fear.

It's important to note that anxiety exists on a spectrum, and the specific features and severity can vary greatly from person to person. In some cases, anxiety can escalate to the point of panic attacks, which involve sudden and intense feelings of terror, along with physical symptoms like shortness of breath and chest pain. If anxiety is significantly impacting an individual's daily life, seeking support from a mental health professional is recommended to explore treatment options and develop coping strategies.

A Caregiving Story: Anxiety + Chronic Illness

Anxiety had always been a close companion to Mark. Its unwelcome presence manifested in racing thoughts and a perpetual feeling of unease. He liked to think of it as a motivating force, even if it got in the way at times. Now, as he assumed the role of caregiver for his wife, Lisa, who was battling a chronic illness, his anxiety threatened to overwhelm him.

Caring for someone with a chronic illness meant navigating a maze of medical appointments, medications, and unpredictable health fluctuations. For Mark, each new day brought a fresh wave of anxiety, worrying about the unknown challenges that lay ahead and the tasks that had already piled up.

One sunny morning, Mark sat in the waiting room of the hospital, his hands trembling slightly as he clutched Lisa's medical records and a list of questions for the doctor. The weight of his anxiety bore down on him as he thought about the uncertainties of his wife's condition.

Mark couldn't help but berate himself with self-doubt, thinking, "I should be stronger for her. Why can't I shake this anxiety?" His mind raced with catastrophic scenarios, each more terrifying than the last. The waiting room's sterile walls seemed to close in on him.

Desperate for relief, Mark decided to seek help. He began attending therapy sessions with a counselor who specialized in anxiety and caregiving. In these sessions, he learned strategies to manage his anxiety while providing the best care for Lisa.

One of the techniques his therapist introduced was grounding techniques. Mark started practicing breathing exercises and noticing his surroundings, focusing on the present moment rather than getting lost in anxious thoughts about the future. This newfound skill allowed him to approach caregiving with a sense of calm and presence with increasing frequency.

His therapist also worked with him on his thoughts, which were often repetitive and focused on unlikely scenarios or things he couldn't control, like obscure symptoms springing up suddenly and his wife feeling depressed because of her poor health. Gradually, he gained proficiency in identifying the self-critic in his thinking and shifting focus to those things within his control. Over time, his anxious thoughts became less impactful and less

> frequent. He still had days where his mind would get away from him, but he was swifter to reel it back in.
>
> He learned to acknowledge his anxiety without judgment and to be kind to himself in moments of doubt. Mark found solace in the love and resilience that bound him to Lisa. He realized that his anxiety was just one facet of his being and that, despite its presence, he was capable of providing the unwavering support and care that his wife needed.

What about 'Good' Anxiety?

Anxiety brings excessive worry, fear, and apprehension about future events. Caregiving, with its inherent uncertainties and responsibilities, provides a context ripe for anxiety. With the right approach, the activities of caregiving can be both challenging and rewarding for individuals dealing with anxiety. You might be a person who thinks of anxiety as a performance enhancing drug, as if enough worry will make us conscientious or productive. This is only partially true.

We have a certain level of stress that is good for performance. There is a graphical concept called the Yerkes-Dodson curve, which shows that for many tasks and people, performance actually improves with *initial* increases in stress. This stress could be considered arousing stress, or the stress needed to be awake and engaged in a task. Think for example about a task with a distant deadline; you're likely not too motivated to engage in it. But as the deadline approaches, you feel more interested and motivated. This is that *initial* anxiety that can be good. However, if stress continues to grow, say, if the deadline is too close for comfort, then we get frantic and begin to do poorly. Our attention becomes splintered by too much stress. This split attention can make us more error prone. If this type of stress goes on for too long, our health can be impacted, especially if the stress is unrelenting. Eleven percent of family caregivers report declines in physical health attributed to caregiving, and this decline is proportional to how many Activities of Daily Living (ADLs) they perform—such as bathing, managing medications, feeding, etc. (Family Caregiver Alliance, n.d.). Basically, more caregiving tasks to worry about. So, when we talk about anxiety, we're talking about the kind of thinking or physical stress that is beyond that needed for optimal performance.

Another facet to anxiety is perspective or mindset. The way we perceive a task can be either as a challenge that is at the edge of our abilities or a threat that feels out of our control. This means that we can be spurred into action out of a sense of accomplishment or out of a sense of fear. Think of it as running towards something or running away from something—either way you're running, but one way is much more enjoyable. You've likely correctly guessed that the latter, threat-based action, is going to be less pleasant and more detrimental. Our bodies take an energetic hit, even for good experiences, which is why we need to sleep at the end of even the best day. Threat-based action has a different physiologic reaction in the body, one that is harder on the system both physically and chemically. The aim is to make the outcome of taking action be low impact, as efficient as possible. Difficult things are challenging, but they don't need to be frightening. For this reason, if we can reframe the demands of caregiving in a way that they can be perceived as a challenge, we can experience something as difficult yet rewarding. I'm not going to pretend that any or all tasks only need the right lighting to make them enjoyable. That's not the case. But we can shift many tasks of caregiving into a light that lends more ease in doing them.

The Thinking & Feeling Part

Here are some solutions for the internal behaviors caregivers with anxiety can experience, such as unhelpful thought patterns or overwhelming feelings. Our thoughts impact our feelings and vis-versa, so we're lumping them together here for one big bag of solutions. Some of these would be considered Cognitive-Behavioral Therapy interventions, which is a fancy label for ways of working with your thoughts and behaviors.

- **Focus on What You Can Control**: One of the hallmark features of anxiety is excessive, often irrational worry about various aspects of life. Anxiety often comes from a sense of uncertainty and feeling out of control. It's easy to find reasons to worry when caregiving. Almost 30% of family caregivers are afraid of making a mistake, with the most fear being about making mistakes in managing medications, using meters and monitors, and performing wound care (AARP, 2020). Rumination (i.e., reviewing the same worry over and over) can feel like we are gathering information when we're actually spinning our wheels. It's quite draining, but often occurs on tasks that are uncertain (e.g., "Will the doctor reply to my question about their medication?"). Let's review some ways to better relate to control/uncertainty:

- <u>Identify What IS Within Your Control:</u> Start by distinguishing between what you can and cannot control. For instance, you can control your responses, actions, and attitudes, but you might not be able to control the progression of a loved one's illness. Or, you can take the initiative to learn more about the care recipient's condition or treatment options, but cannot control how the care recipient feels or reacts. Like Mark and his anxiety over the unknown, you can also shift towards the tasks in front of you rather than speculate about the unknown variables that *might* crop up in the future.

- <u>No Crystal Ball:</u> Remind yourself we can only make decisions with the information available to use at the time—then give yourself some parameters on when you will stop gathering information. After you make a decision, if something goes wrong, remind yourself that you made a decision based on the information you had at the time, and you chose what seemed best based on that information. Go easy on yourself. You can also rely more on trusted experts instead of gathering more information yourself. For example, instead of you doing all the research about a treatment, you may be able to simply ask the doctor which treatments they recommend and why, relying on their knowledge.

- <u>Focus on Your Responses</u>: While you can't control everything that happens, you can control how you respond. Develop healthy coping mechanisms for stress and challenges, like pausing for a breath or taking a quick break before replying to an emotionally-charged situation. If a situation is not within your control, consciously redirect your attention to actions or thoughts that are within your control.

- <u>Prioritize Self-Care</u>: Shift focus to activities within your control, like activities that nurture your health, such as exercise, proper nutrition, and sufficient rest.

- <u>Let Go of the Need for Perfection</u>: Understand that seeking perfection often involves trying to control uncontrollable factors. Embrace imperfection and focus on doing your best within the controllable parameters. You can adapt as new information becomes available; there is no need to beat yourself up as if you could have known something you didn't.

- <u>Journaling</u>: Keep a journal to reflect on your daily experiences, focusing on what you were able to control and how you responded to uncontrollable events.

- **Intrusive Thoughts**: Intrusive and distressing thoughts, often related to fears or negative outcomes, can be a common feature of anxiety. These thoughts can become obsessive and hard to shake off, making it difficult to focus on other tasks. Intrusive thoughts about potential negative outcomes for the person one is caring for can be distracting and emotionally draining.

  - Acknowledge these thoughts without judgment and then redirect focus to more constructive tasks. Mindfulness meditation can help in managing these thoughts. See the section on OCD for other useful strategies.

- **Break the Loop**: People with anxiety may engage in overthinking and rumination. Rumination is repeatedly reviewing past events or worries about future ones. This can lead caregivers to constantly second-guess their caregiving decisions, creating a cycle of doubt and increased anxiety.

  - Set aside a specific time for reflection, and outside of that time, consciously redirect thoughts to present activities. E.g., set a 10-minute timer and unleash that inner worrier, write down those concerns, then set them aside.

  - Practicing mindfulness can also be helpful here.

- When you're ruminating about something negative that happened or that you did, try mixing in memories of things that went well or things you did right. This can sometimes help break the repetitive negative loop.

- **Play the Odds**: Imagining the worst-case scenarios, even when they are unlikely, can amplify anxiety and stress. It can also make caregivers overly cautious or hesitant, potentially leading to overprotective behaviors or unnecessary interventions. E.g., avoiding walks in the park with a care recipient who has mobility issues because you imagine them having a severe fall.

  - Challenge catastrophic thoughts by considering more realistic outcomes and probabilities. Keeping a journal to record these thoughts and reality-testing them can be beneficial.

- **Avoid Avoidance**: Avoidance of decisions or tasks is so appealing in the short run, but can wreak havoc in the long term. Procrastination can be a feature of anxiety, as the fear of not meeting one's own or others' expectations can be paralyzing. Fear of making mistakes might cause caregivers to delay important tasks or decisions, which can be detrimental to both the caregiver and the person being cared for. To avoid avoidance, gradually expose yourself to the tasks or situations you tend to avoid, starting with less challenging ones or a very tiny subtask. This helps build confidence and reduce anxiety over time. See the section on ADHD for more strategies (page 3).

- **Practice Positive Self-talk:** Replace negative and anxious thoughts with positive affirmations. Remind yourself of your strengths and the important role you are playing in your loved one's life. Try setting aside a time each morning to write down 5 things that went well in your caretaking yesterday. Remember, don't just focus on the big or obvious events, even something as routine as making yourself a warm cup of tea in the morning can be a positive success you reflect on.

- **See Bloopers and Highlights:** It can be challenging to figure out what "good enough" means, especially when we compare ourselves to others. Social media often shows the "highlight reels" of caregiving—the picture-perfect moments, achievements, or smiling faces. Similarly, when talking to friends or other caregivers, we might only see their best moments and not the "bloopers"—the struggles, missteps, or tough times that everyone experiences. To gain a more balanced perspective, remind yourself that your caregiving has its own mix of highlights and bloopers, just like everyone else's. Focus on the meaningful ways you show up, even when things don't go perfectly. "Good enough" isn't about having a flawless highlight reel; it's about consistently showing care, love, and effort, even in the blooper moments. Recognizing this can help you feel less pressure to measure up to an ideal that doesn't reflect reality. Focus on the process rather than the outcome and celebrate small achievements. (See the following section on Perfectionism for more detailed tips on this.)

- **Social Resilience**: Fear of negative judgment from others or simply a busy schedule can lead to social withdrawal. Withdrawal from social activities can lead to isolation for both the caregiver and the person being cared for, reducing their support network and satisfaction of social needs.

  - Remind yourself that *you* are likely your biggest critic.

  - Ask yourself what evidence you have that others will judge you. Is it possible you're making assumptions or trying to read their minds? Often, these fears are not based on reality.

  - Try to maintain social connections, even if it's just through phone calls or digital means. Social support is crucial for emotional well-being. See page 28 for an example of how to reach out to a friend to increase your contact with them.

- **Recognize Your Feelings**: Understand that it's normal to feel anxious or stressed as a caregiver. Acknowledge these feelings instead of suppressing them. This is the first step in managing anxiety.

- **Ground Out Panic**: You may experience a panic attack (e.g., sudden and intense feelings of terror, shortness of breath, and chest pain). Panic attacks can incapacitate caregivers temporarily, making them unable to provide care during these episodes. Learn and practice grounding and/or breathing techniques designed for panic attacks. For example, Box Breathing–inhale for a count of four, hold your breath for four counts, exhale for four counts, and then wait for four counts before inhaling again. You can visualize drawing one side of a box on each count of four. This structured breathing can help regulate your breath and calm your nervous system. Learn to recognize the early signs of a panic attack (e.g., fear, physical tension, or hypervigilance) and have a plan in place for managing them, such as a safe, quiet space to recover.

The Doing Part

A lot of what we have talked about has been focused on managing what goes on inside our heads. Here are some solutions tailored to more external behaviors caregivers with anxiety can engage in to resolve the impact of anxiety on their wellbeing and effectiveness in everyday activities:

1. **Set Up for Sleep**: Many people with anxiety experience difficulty falling asleep or staying asleep due to racing thoughts or physical discomfort. This in turn can impact their alertness and patience.

    a. Worry-dump right before bed: write down all the things you might think about if you wake up in the middle of the night, then set a time the next day to review the list (even if you don't review it, your mind thinks you will and will leave you alone). End by writing down one or two things that brought you joy that day.

b. Create a calming bedtime routine (including that worry-dump) and ensure a comfortable sleep environment. Avoid caffeine and screen time before bed, and consider relaxation techniques if you have trouble sleeping.

c. Try meditation exercises. There are free apps such as CBTi that allow you to play a script that guides you through a meditation.

d. If your thoughts won't quite budge, you can try playing a podcast or audiobook. Try choosing one that is interesting enough to keep you focused on it instead of your thoughts, but one that is not too exciting, as this can keep you up. Notice, these recommendations include audio-only formats. It is best to avoid television as the light from the TV can make it harder to sleep.

2. **Get Physical**: Anxiety's physical symptoms, such as muscle tension or shallow breathing, are the body's way of preparing for perceived threat or danger. They're also exhausting. This makes it hard for caregivers to recharge, reducing their effectiveness and increasing the risk of caregiver burnout.

a. Address muscle tension through body awareness; practice by setting a timer for 5 minutes that cues you to check in and drop your shoulders or relax your jaw. Repeat the exercise a few times, or as long as you'd like.

b. Burn off stress hormones with regular physical exercise or yoga.

c. Use exercises designed to reverse tension that comes from anxiety. Deep breathing exercises and relaxation techniques like progressive muscle relaxation are easy to find on a quick web search of "progressive muscle relaxation" or go to doctorolson.com/media

3. **Organize and Relax**: The demands of caregiving can be amplified by anxiety from disorganization, potentially leading to feelings of helplessness and ineffectiveness. Keep caregiving tasks, appointments, and medical information well-organized. This can reduce the anxiety that comes from feeling overwhelmed or unprepared.

4. **Tiny Chunks:** It can be challenging for people with anxiety to concentrate and stay focused due to racing thoughts and worries. Break tasks into smaller chunks and focus on one thing at a time (e.g., one phone call, identifying times available for future appointments, one medication adjustment, etc.). Set a timer and focus on that one small task for the next 5 minutes.

5. **Checks and balances:** Cognitive effects of stress and multitasking demands can make caregivers more error prone. This is particularly the case with individuals

experiencing anxiety as well. Having a system of checks and balances can improve accuracy. Checks and balances just means finding ways to check in about the accuracy of your execution. This might look like consulting with healthcare professionals to review your care plan, or simply reviewing your own tasks completed each day. For example, if you're forgetful of important tasks when leaving the home, make a list to tape by your front door (e.g., lock doors, turn off the stove), then check the list as you leave. Just like that, your accuracy (and frustration) can improve.

6. **Set Realistic Goals**: One style of goal setting is called "SMART" goals: Specific, Measurable, Achievable, Relevant, and Time-Bound.

   a. <u>Specific</u>: Rather than a vague goal like "get fit," specify what aspect of fitness you want to improve. For instance, "I want to increase my stamina and strength to handle caregiving tasks more efficiently."

   b. <u>Measurable</u>: Determine how you will measure your progress. "I will measure my progress by being able to complete a 15-minute workout without feeling overly fatigued and by being able to lift 20 pounds easily."

   c. <u>Achievable</u>: Ensure the goal is realistic. "Given my current fitness level and caregiving responsibilities, a 15-minute workout is an achievable target."

d. <u>Relevant</u>: The goal should be meaningful and beneficial to your life. "Improving my physical fitness is relevant as it will make caregiving tasks easier and improve my overall health."

e. <u>Time-bound</u>: Set a deadline to achieve the goal. "I aim to achieve this level of fitness within the next three months."

7. **Establish Boundaries**: Set clear boundaries about what you can and cannot do. It's important to balance caregiving with your own needs and responsibilities. You may need to engage in a little assertiveness training to practice speaking your mind directly, yet respectfully; for example, being assertive about using a Hoyer lift might go something like this: "I understand that you are uncomfortable with using the Hoyer lift, but my priority is to ensure your safety and mine during transfers. This lift minimizes the risk of injury for you and my back so I can continue providing the care you need." Also, read about creating a Caregiver Container on page 167.

8. **Schedule Time for Yourself**: Regularly schedule time away from caregiving duties (I know, when?) to relax and engage in activities you enjoy. This personal time is vital for your mental health.

a. Take regular, brief breaks to avoid anxiety build up over time. Many people experience reduced stress within just a few minutes, sometimes referred to as a "micro-break" (Kim et al., 2019; Helton, et al., 2017). That is all it takes sometimes.

b. In fact, studies have shown taking breaks is like creating time for yourself (e.g., after a 20- to 30-minute break students performed as though they had 19 additional days of schooling; Sievertsen et al., 2016). I think we could all use more time.

9. **Educate Yourself**: The more you know about your loved one's condition and the nature of caregiving, the more competent and confident you may feel. This can help alleviate anxiety stemming from uncertainty or lack of knowledge. Ask their healthcare team or simply, with caution, the Internet.

10. **Use Technology and Resources**: Utilize apps and online resources designed for caregivers. They can help manage tasks and provide useful information, reducing some of the stress and anxiety associated with caregiving. (See Technology section on page 184.)

Gauging Care Alignment

For some of us, the more data we have on how we're doing, the more relaxed we feel. Data can help us adapt, improvise, and overcome possible misalignments or oversights in care, and rest assured that things are generally in the target area. One such tool is the Values and Preferences Scale (Whitlatch, Feinberg, & Tucke, 2005). It's designed to highlight areas that one side of the caregiving relationship feels is more or less important than the other. With this information, you can then adjust your approach on tasks to optimize alignment, such as opting for more time connecting with family members and less on finances. The scale is completed separately by the caregiver and the care recipient, with differences in ratings pointing to helpful adjustments in care. You can complete the interactive questionnaire at doctorolson.com/care for immediate results. If you complete the questionnaire using the above link, you'll be provided with suggested communication strategies, possible adjustments, and other tips.

Silver Linings

While anxiety can be challenging to deal with, there can be hidden perks or silver linings for caregivers facing this condition. Remember, though, while we bring levity to the quirks of anxious caregiving, it's crucial to keep that anxiety in check. And with some planning, many of these perks can be maintained even after resolving anxious tendencies. After all, everyone needs their inner peace more than their inner critic!

1. **Reassuring Routine**: The more routine aspects of caregiving can provide a sense of predictability, potentially reducing anxiety.

2. **Positive Feedback**: Helping others and receiving gratitude can boost self-esteem and counteract negative thoughts.

3. **Self-Care Echo**: Focusing on self-care to manage anxiety can also lead to better caregiving quality. You're essentially a model for how to tend well to those individual needs.

4. **Master of Plan B (and C, and D…)**: Problem-solving is your involuntary mental workout. Your brain is doing emotional push-ups all day, every day, flipping worries into solutions. And yes, it's totally okay to brag about your 'worry-triggered wisdom' at dinner parties. Thanks to your relentless "What if" scenarios, if you incorporate a pause to breathe and reflect, you can have a solid list of backup plans for all those possible scenarios. Anxiety often leads to rigorous planning and preparation. Caregivers with anxiety may excel in organizing and ensuring that all caregiving tasks are effectively managed. *Note: See initial section titled "A Note on Anxiety" for clarification.*

5. **On-point Communication**: You might engage in check-ins, updates, and chats that may initially be prompted by your anxiety. Anxiety can lead to hyperawareness of potential misunderstandings, motivating caregivers to communicate more clearly and effectively. You keep everyone in the loop so well, you could give the postal service a run for its money.

6. **Heightened Empathy**: Anxiety can make individuals more sensitive to the emotional needs of those they care for. This heightened empathy allows caregivers

to provide exceptional emotional support. Anxiety can make caregivers more attuned to subtle changes in their loved one's well-being, allowing for early detection of health issues or changes in behavior.

7. **Effective Advocacy**: Caregivers with anxiety may be more assertive when advocating for their loved one's needs within the healthcare system, ensuring they receive the best care.

8. **Valuing Moments of Calm**: Anxiety can help caregivers cherish and create moments of calm and serenity, which can be especially meaningful for both the caregiver and the care recipient. Seeking soothing music, creating a few minutes of silence or meditation, and other restorative activities can help both caregivers and care recipients alike.

It's essential to remember that while there can be hidden perks, overall caregivers with anxiety face an added challenge. Further, most symptoms of anxiety are quite treatable, meaning you can address the downside of anxiety and keep the high level of performance sans anxiety. It's about knowing what drives your unique (and at times quite universal) concerns and how to motivate and cue yourself with systems designed to give confidence, thereby resolving anxieties. Other times, it's responding to your inner critic effectively (see section on depression, page 21). And of course, seeking support, self-care, and professional help when necessary are crucial steps to navigate caregiving with anxiety.

OCD: Shifting the Rituals of Care

"Enough is as good as a feast."

– An old English proverb

The sights, sounds, and smells of caregiving can be a bit much for even the strongest of stomachs. Add on a tendency to revisit these experiences over and over and over, and well, you get the idea. However, caregiving, with its fluid nature and unforeseen challenges, can clash with the structured world of someone with OCD. In this chapter, we delve into obsessive-compulsive disorder (OCD) and caregiving, a space marked by a desire for control and predictability among caregiving's inherent unpredictability. For caregivers grappling with OCD, their world is often one of meticulous order, where routines and rituals provide a sense of security.

Core Symptoms of OCD

Obsessions: Persistent, unwanted thoughts or images that cause distress or anxiety.

- For caregivers, these might include worries about contamination, making a mistake in medication administration, or the health of their loved one.

- It is not uncommon for individuals to experience thoughts of harming others accidentally, and at times even fear of doing so purposefully, despite no actual intention to do so.

Compulsions: Repetitive behaviors or mental acts that a person feels driven to perform in response to an obsession.

- In caregiving, this might manifest as excessive cleaning, repeatedly checking on the care recipient, or constantly seeking reassurance about caregiving tasks.

Avoidance: Avoiding situations or activities that trigger obsessions.

- This can limit the caregiver's ability to provide comprehensive care if they avoid certain tasks or environments.

Additional OCD Symptoms

Hyper-Responsibility: A sense of exaggerated responsibility for the care recipient's well-being is common, with thoughts like, "Their health is entirely in my hands."

- *Tip*: Regularly remind yourself that you are one part of the care recipient's support system, not the entirety of it. Run ideas by others in their care team to provide you a sense of support and distributed responsibility.

Need for Reassurance: Constantly seeking validation or reassurance about their caregiving decisions, which can be time-consuming and mentally exhausting.

- *Tip*: Limit the number of times you allow yourself to seek reassurance. Gradually reduce this over time to become more comfortable with your decisions.

Rigidity: Struggling with flexibility, which is often necessary in the dynamic environment of caregiving.

- *Tip*: Develop caregiving plans that include alternative options. This approach helps in adapting to unexpected changes and reduces anxiety associated with deviations from the plan.

A Caregiving Story: OCD + Disability

OCD had long been a presence in Alex's life. Its unrelenting grip manifested in obsessive thoughts and compulsive rituals that seemed impossible to escape. Now, as he stepped into the role of caregiver for his sister, Lily, who had a physical disability, his OCD tendencies threatened to overwhelm him.

Caring for someone with a physical disability meant navigating a complex landscape of mobility challenges, accessibility needs, and constant attention to detail. For Alex, each day seemed like a never-ending loop of checking, rechecking, and arranging things precisely.

One morning, as Alex helped Lily with her morning routine, he noticed that the wheels of her wheelchair were not perfectly aligned. His heart raced, and his anxiety skyrocketed as he felt an overwhelming urge to fix them. He knew that Lily relied on the wheelchair for her mobility, and any imperfection felt like a catastrophe.

The weight of his OCD bore down on him, and self-critical thoughts flooded his mind. "I should be better at managing these compulsions. Lily deserves better than this," he thought, berating himself for his perceived shortcomings as a caregiver.

Recognizing the toll his OCD was taking on his ability to provide care, Alex decided it was time to seek professional help. He began attending therapy sessions with a psychologist who specialized in caregiving. In these sessions, he learned strategies to manage his obsessive thoughts and compulsive behaviors while ensuring Lily's well-being.

One of the techniques his therapist introduced was cognitive-behavioral therapy (CBT), which helped Alex challenge and reframe his obsessive thoughts. He gradually learned to resist the urge to give in to his compulsions and to tolerate the discomfort of uncertainty, all while providing the care for Lily.

Additionally, Alex joined a support group for caregivers of individuals with physical disabilities. There, he connected with others who understood the unique challenges he faced. Sharing his experiences and hearing their stories provided validation that precision in some tasks can't be top priority, He also felt a sense of belonging.

As he continued to care for Lily, Alex discovered the power of self-compassion. He realized that his OCD tendencies did not define his worth as a caregiver. He understood that caregiving was a journey filled with complexities, and his struggles with OCD were just one aspect of it.

Through the trials of caregiving, Alex found solace in the love and dedication he had for Lily. He understood that while his OCD posed challenges, it did not diminish his ability to provide compassionate and attentive care. While still tending toward high standards, he focused on defining and adhering to the limits of "good enough" when completing tasks—inspired by the phrase "enough is as good as a feast." He also grew in his ability to highlight the moments of connection and shared love, recognizing that they were the most important aspects of their journey together.

Their path was far from easy, but it became a journey of self-discovery and resilience for Alex. He learned that his OCD tendencies did not have to dictate his actions as a caregiver, and he could strike a balance between his need for order and the needs of his sister. In their shared moments of strength and vulnerability, they found a deeper connection that carried them through the unique challenges of caregiving.

Some Specific Solutions

Below are brief solutions to a handful of specific issues experienced by caregivers affected by OCD. Confronting and stopping the OCD behavior is the best way to improve symptoms long term. However, some people are not ready for treatment, or are focused on urgent responsibilities and only interested in strategies to get them through the day. Some strategies offered here may help ease distress in the moment; however, keep in mind that focusing only on what gets you through the now may negatively affect your symptoms in the long term. So, when you are ready, targeted treatment is the best approach for dealing with the symptoms in the long term.

1. **Gradual Flexibility:** Struggling with changes in caregiving routines or plans? Gradually introduce flexibility/alternatives in routines and practice adapting to changes.

2. **Real Health Info**: For excessive worry about germs or illness, leading to over-sanitization, educate yourself about realistic hygiene practices and set boundaries for cleaning activities.

3. **Perfectly Imperfect**: Striving for perfection in caregiving tasks can lead to stress and burnout. Set realistic standards and remind oneself that it's okay to be 'good enough.'

4. **Reason out Importance**: Challenges in prioritizing tasks due to obsessions or compulsions. Use time management techniques and prioritize tasks based on importance and urgency. See the prioritization tips under Versatile Strategies on page 166.

Cognitive Behavioral Strategies

Cognitive Behavioral Therapy (CBT) techniques, possibly under the guidance of a therapist, can be effective in challenging and changing compulsive behaviors. A therapist will typically tailor these techniques to the individual's specific symptoms, severity, and personal circumstances. CBT for OCD is usually a structured process, with gradual progression and ongoing assessment of progress. A therapist specializing in CBT would likely suggest a combination of the following techniques:

1. **Exposure and Response Prevention (ERP)**: This is a core approach in treating OCD. It involves gradually exposing the patient to feared objects or ideas (exposure) and teaching them to resist the urge to perform compulsive rituals in response (response prevention). Caregivers with OCD might have compulsions directly related to their caregiving duties, such as excessive cleaning, or excessive re-checking on the care recipient or medication count. Using ERP, they can gradually expose themselves to their anxiety triggers (e.g., not checking on the care recipient immediately when the urge arises) and practice delaying or avoiding the compulsive response under controlled conditions, perhaps with the support of a therapist. (See example further on in this chapter on having healthcare workers in the home.)

2. **Cognitive Restructuring**: Cognitive restructuring is a powerful tool for managing persistent fears or irrational

beliefs that interfere with the ability to stay present and complete tasks effectively. It shifts the thinker's relationship with the thought and changes the thought itself. For example, a caregiver might think, "What if I gave the wrong dose? I need to check again to make sure," even after confirming multiple times. This pattern of re-checking can consume significant time and mental energy, leaving the caregiver feeling trapped in a cycle of doubt and fear. These thoughts, while rooted in care and responsibility, can make it difficult to focus on other tasks or remain emotionally present.

Through cognitive restructuring with a therapist, caregivers learn to challenge and reframe these unhelpful thoughts. In the example of re-checking medication, the caregiver might replace the thought, "If I don't check one more time, I could harm them," with, "I followed the correct procedure, and repeated checking won't add safety—it's my anxiety speaking." This reframing helps reduce the compulsion to re-check, freeing the caregiver from the cycle of doubt. By addressing these obsessive tendencies, cognitive restructuring allows caregivers to regain a sense of trust in their actions, enabling them to manage their responsibilities with greater confidence and emotional balance.

3. **Mindfulness-Based Cognitive Therapy**: This approach combines cognitive therapy with mindfulness strategies. It helps patients observe their thoughts and

feelings without judgment and without immediately reacting to them.

4. **Behavioral Experiments**: These are practical exercises where patients test the accuracy of their obsessive thoughts in a controlled setting, learning to gauge the realistic likelihood of their feared outcomes. Caregivers can design experiments to test the validity of their OCD fears in a caregiving context, such as the fear that not performing a ritual will result in negative consequences for the care recipient. By observing that not engaging in the compulsion does not lead to the feared outcome, they can begin to dismantle the belief fueling their OCD symptoms.

5. **Habit Reversal Training**: This technique is particularly useful for compulsive behaviors. It involves learning to recognize the onset of a compulsive urge and then substituting a different response that is incompatible with the compulsion. For instance, if a caregiver feels the urge to repeatedly check if medical equipment is working, they could replace this with a single check followed by a different, incompatible action, like writing in a care log.

6. **Assertiveness Training**: This helps patients learn to express their needs and boundaries clearly, which can be beneficial in managing OCD-related stress and improving interpersonal relationships. This can be beneficial in situations where caregivers need to communicate their own needs or boundaries, especially

when OCD symptoms might demand more time or energy than they can afford. Learning to assertively communicate can help manage their condition while still attending to the needs of the care recipient.

7. **Problem-Solving Skills**: Developing effective problem-solving strategies can help patients deal with OCD symptoms and related life challenges in a more constructive manner. Developing strategies to address both caregiving challenges and OCD symptoms can enhance a caregiver's ability to cope. For instance, if obsessive fears about the care recipient's health are prominent, the caregiver can consult with their healthcare provider to determine how often monitoring actually needs to occur. Then strategize a time where checking is indeed helpful based on medical recommendations. If medical recommendations aren't enough to have you stop there, explore other ways to reduce checks, like habit reversal training. When you haven't engaged in the checking behavior that day or you have done so much less, ask yourself, did the feared thing happen? Emphasize for yourself that the outcome of not checking was positive. Give yourself a little reward even.

Check Yourself

For caregivers affected by OCD, especially those with a tendency towards repetitive behaviors, setting limits can be a crucial part of managing symptoms while providing effective care. Repetitive behaviors, such as excessive handwashing or taking overly long showers, can arise from anxiety or obsessive tendencies, making daily caregiving tasks more challenging. Setting limits can help manage these behaviors effectively. Consider the strategies below for managing symptoms. Note: While helpful with some symptoms, this is not advice for *treating* OCD; consulting with a mental health professional will allow for tailored treatment plans to each person's unique needs. If already in treatment, check with your provider to ensure these techniques are best for your situation.

1. **Scheduled Check-Ins**: Set specific times for checking tasks that need regular attention, such as medication administration or safety-related concerns. Limit these checks to a reasonable number per day.

2. **Use of Checklists**: Create a checklist for daily tasks. Once a task is completed and checked off, resist the urge to recheck. The visual confirmation can help reassure that the task is done.

3. **Timed Checks**: If repetitive checking is a concern, allocate a specific amount of time for each checking task. Use a timer to adhere to these limits.

4. **Gradual Reduction of Checks**: Gradually reduce the frequency of checks over time. Start by slightly decreasing the number of checks or the time spent checking, and then progressively reduce it further.

5. **Log It**: Keep a log to track your checking behaviors and your progress in managing them. This can provide insights into patterns and triggers.

6. **Involve a Support Person**: Discuss your efforts to set limits on checking behaviors with a trusted person who can help hold you accountable and provide support.

7. **Positive Reinforcement**: Reward yourself for adhering to the set limits. This could be through self-praise, a favorite activity, or a small treat.

By implementing these strategies, caregivers with OCD can work towards managing their behaviors more effectively, leading to more joy for themselves and improved care for their loved one. Remember, progress may be gradual, and seeking professional guidance can provide additional support and tailored strategies.

Healthcare Workers in Your Home

For a caregiver with OCD, having healthcare workers in the home can be particularly stressful due to the increased potential for triggers related to OCD symptoms, such as fears about contamination, a need for symmetry, or specific routines being disrupted. Here are some strategies that might help navigate these challenges:

1. **Open Communication**: It's important to communicate your needs and concerns with the healthcare workers who come into your home. You don't have to disclose your diagnosis if you're not comfortable doing so, but

explaining certain preferences or requirements you have for maintaining your mental health can help. For instance, you might request that they follow specific hygiene practices or notify you before making changes in the environment.

2. **Educate the Healthcare Workers**: If you do feel comfortable disclosing your OCD, try also educating. General information about OCD can help them understand your actions and needs better. This doesn't mean you need to share your personal experiences, but rather general information about OCD that might help them be more mindful of their actions in your home.

3. **Establish Clear Boundaries and Routines**: Work with healthcare workers to establish routines and boundaries that respect your needs and their professional responsibilities. This might include setting specific times for visits, arranging the house in a certain way, or having designated areas for the healthcare workers to use. This can help minimize uncertainty and reduce anxiety.

4. **Create a Safe Space**: Designate an area in your home as a 'safe space' that is off-limits to healthcare workers. This space can be a sanctuary where you can retreat to when feeling overwhelmed, ensuring you have a place where your environment remains controlled and reassuring.

5. **Practice Stress-Relief Techniques**: Engage in stress-relief practices such as deep breathing exercises, meditation, mindfulness, or gentle physical activity. These techniques can help manage anxiety levels when they start to rise, providing a way to cope with the presence of healthcare workers in your home.

6. **Seek Support**: Having a therapist or a support group can provide an outlet for discussing your experiences and feelings. If you're already seeing a therapist for OCD, discuss these specific challenges with them. They can offer tailored strategies to cope with the stress of having healthcare workers in your home.

7. **Gradual Exposure**: With professional guidance, gradually exposing yourself to the stressors related to healthcare workers in your home can decrease your sensitivity over time. Ideally, this can be done under the guidance of a mental health professional experienced in treating OCD. (See a step-by-step example at the end of this section.)

8. **Maintain Your Treatment Regimen**: If you have one, ensure you're adhering to your prescribed treatment regimen, whether it involves medication, therapy, or both. Consistently managing your OCD symptoms is key to handling additional stressors.

9. **Adjust Expectations**: Acknowledge that it's okay for things not to be perfect. Part of dealing with OCD involves learning to tolerate discomfort and uncertainty.

Working on adjusting your expectations and practicing acceptance can be beneficial.

10. **Have a Contingency Plan**: Knowing in advance what steps to take if anxiety becomes overwhelming can be reassuring. This might include having a friend or family member you can call, a relaxation technique you can use, or a signal to healthcare workers that you need a break.

An Example of Gradual Exposure

Gradual exposure, or desensitization, is a therapeutic technique where you gradually expose yourself to the source of your anxiety in a controlled, step-by-step process. The exact steps are collaboratively designed by you and your healthcare provider. This method can be especially useful for caregivers who feel overwhelmed or anxious about having healthcare workers in their home to assist with caregiving duties.

Throughout this process, it's beneficial to monitor your feelings and stress levels, adjusting the pace as needed. Gradual exposure is not about rushing but about gently easing into the situation until your initial anxiety or discomfort becomes manageable or even disappears.

Here's an example of how gradual exposure might look in this context:

Step 1: Start with Visualization

Begin by visualizing healthcare workers coming into your home. Imagine the process in detail, from their arrival to the caregiving tasks they perform. Spend a few minutes each day picturing this scenario, aiming to become more comfortable with the thought over time.

Step 2: Gather Information

Research or speak to the healthcare agency about the specific roles and routines of healthcare workers. Understanding their procedures and what to expect can help reduce anxiety. You might even request photos or brief bios of the staff if available, to familiarize yourself with them before they enter your home.

Step 3: Virtual Introduction

Arrange for a video call with the healthcare worker(s) who will be assisting in your home. This allows you to meet them in a low-pressure environment, ask questions, and start building a rapport.

Step 4: Short Visits

Schedule the first few visits to be short, with specific, limited tasks. Being present during these visits can help you gradually acclimate to having others in your home and involved in caregiving.

Step 5: Gradually Extend the Time

As your comfort level increases, gradually extend the duration of the healthcare workers' visits or expand the range of tasks they perform.

Step 6: Partial Presence

Start staying only part of the time during the healthcare workers' visits, perhaps stepping out for a short walk or engaging in another activity in a different part of the home.

Step 7: Full Transition

Eventually, allow yourself to leave the house or engage fully in your own activities while the healthcare worker is there, trusting that your loved one is in good hands.

Working with a therapist to help gauge target behaviors, incremental advances in intensity, and pacing of steps is often critical to success. The steps above are simply to give an idea of what it might look like to engage in a gradual exposure intervention.

Silver Linings

Despite the challenges, there are silver linings to the experience of caregiving with OCD. These include:

1. **Attention to Detail:** The meticulous nature of OCD can be an asset in managing complex caregiving tasks.

2. **Structured Routines**: Creating structured routines can provide stability and predictability for both the caregiver and the care recipient.

3. **High Standards of Care**: A desire for perfection can lead to a high standard of care and thoroughness in caregiving tasks.

4. **Empathy and Understanding**: Personal struggles with OCD can foster empathy and a deeper understanding of the care recipient's needs.

5. **Positive Feedback**: Receiving gratitude and appreciation from the care recipient or others involved in their care can offer a sense of accomplishment and alleviate anxiety.

Caregiving while managing OCD requires patience and tools. Caregivers with OCD can discover their strengths, develop new coping strategies, and find a sense of fulfillment in their role. Remember, seeking help and building a supportive network are helpful steps in navigating this journey successfully.

Addiction: Balancing Recovery and Care

"The greatest gift you can give your family

and the world is a healthy you."

- Joyce Meyer

The demands of caregiving impact the recovery process in both positive and negative ways. Addiction, whether it involves substances like alcohol or drugs, or behavioral addictions such as gambling, can significantly impact both the individual and their ability to provide care. Even if you've relapsed, there is still hope and potential for a shift towards recovery. While we won't take a deep-dive into coping strategies, we will cover aspects which connect with addiction in the context of caregiving. We'll also cover handling conflicts and difficult emotions, both within family dynamics and internally within oneself, something that can be important as a caregiver and as a person in recovery.

Core Symptoms of Addiction

The core symptoms of addiction, which can manifest in behaviors related to substance use or other compulsive behaviors, include:

Cravings: Strong and often overwhelming desire or urge to use the substance or engage in addictive behavior.

Loss of Control: Inability to limit the use of a substance or engagement in behavior, despite intentions to stop or cut back, and despite negative consequences, such as deteriorating health, strained relationships, or financial problems.

Physical Dependence & Tolerance: The body adapts to the substance, leading to withdrawal symptoms when use is reduced or stopped. Tolerance occurs when increasing amounts of the substance are needed to achieve the same effect, indicating the body's adaptation to its presence.

It's important to note that the manifestation and intensity of these symptoms can vary widely among individuals. Other symptoms of addiction can be and often are present, including neglecting responsibilities, engaging in risky behavior, loss of interest in activities, and spending excessive time obtaining or recovering from substance use. Addiction is a complex condition, often requiring professional evaluation and treatment.

A Caregiving Story: Healthy Habits

John had always been his father's pillar of strength. He was in his late 40s when his father was diagnosed with a degenerative neurological condition. John naturally stepped into the role of caregiver. However, this new responsibility arrived at a time when John was experiencing a growing dependency on alcohol.

Each day, John oscillated between his commitment to his father and his own inner turmoil. He would start his mornings with a promise to stay sober, only to find himself reaching for a bottle by the evening, seeking solace from the relentless stress and emotional weight of caregiving. His addiction, once a distant concern, had insidiously woven itself into the fabric of his daily life.

One evening, after missing an important doctor's appointment for his father due to a hangover, John confronted the harsh reality of his situation. The guilt and shame that enveloped him were overwhelming. He realized that his struggle with addiction was not just his own battle anymore; it was directly impacting the well-being of his father.

In this moment of clarity, John felt a surge of determination. He understood that to be the caregiver his father deserved, he needed to confront his addiction head-on. This marked the beginning of John's journey towards recovery, a path riddled with challenges but illuminated by the desire to provide consistent care for his father and the potential for waking up feeling good.

John's first step was seeking professional help. He started attending therapy sessions, where he delved into the underlying reasons for his addiction. These sessions were emotionally taxing but cathartic. He uncovered layers of unresolved grief and stress that he had been numbing with alcohol.

Parallel to therapy, John joined a support group for caregivers. Here, he found a community of individuals who resonated with his struggles. Their stories and encouragement provided John with a sense of belonging and understanding that he had long missed.

John's journey was not linear. There were days when the urge to escape into the numbness of alcohol was overwhelming. Instances of his father's health deteriorating served as triggers, sending John into a spiral of guilt and temptation. However, the coping strategies he learned in therapy, combined with the support from his group, led to relapses being shorter and less frequent.

As John progressed in his recovery, his approach to caregiving transformed. While caregiving never became his favorite job, he learned to manage the stressors involved. Being sober helped him be more attentive, which led to more moments of connection with his father. He developed routines for both himself and his father that incorporated healthy habits. Cooking nutritious meals, scheduling regular medical appointments, and engaging in light physical activities became integral parts of their daily lives.

One of the most significant changes in John's life was the re-establishment of trust and a deeper bond with his father. He became more present, not just physically, but emotionally and mentally. His father, who had silently observed John's struggles, expressed pride and gratitude for the changes he saw in his son. This acknowledgment was a powerful motivator for John.

Reflecting on his journey, John recognized the interconnectedness of his recovery and his role as a caregiver. His father's unwavering love and dependence on him gave him a purpose that was larger than his addiction. His struggle and eventual triumph over addiction instilled a sense of resilience and self-awareness that he carried into every aspect of his life.

John's story depicts the raw and real challenges of managing addiction while being a caregiver. Even in the depths of personal struggles, one can find the strength to not only fulfill their duties as a caregiver but also embark on a path of self-recovery and profound personal growth.

The Impact of Caregiving on Recovery

The demands of caregiving can significantly impact addiction recovery, presenting several challenges—as seen below along with solutions bulleted under each:

1. **Limited Time for Recovery Activities**: The time-consuming nature of caregiving responsibilities can limit the individual's ability to attend support group meetings, therapy sessions, or engage in other recovery-related activities.

- Schedule dedicated time for recovery activities, treating them as non-negotiable appointments.

- Explore online or telephone-based support groups and therapy sessions for flexibility.

- Consider obtaining a sponsor for recovery.

2. **Isolation**: Caregivers might find themselves socially isolated due to their responsibilities, reducing their access to supportive networks that are crucial for addiction recovery.

   - Join caregiver support groups, either in-person or online, to connect with others in similar situations.

   - Maintain social connections through regular check-ins with friends and family, even if very brief ("friendship snacks".

3. **Sleep Deprivation and Physical Exhaustion**: The demanding nature of caregiving can lead to irregular sleep patterns and physical exhaustion, both of which can negatively affect mental health and recovery stability.

   - Prioritize sleep hygiene and rest whenever possible; short naps can be remarkably restorative.

   - Reassess your sleep regularly, e.g., monthly or weekly, and adjust or advocate according to your needs.

- ○ Delegate caregiving tasks when needed to allow for rest and recuperation.

4. **Emotional Triggers**: Dealing with the emotional aspects of caregiving, such as the declining health of a loved one, can trigger negative emotions and stress, potentially leading to substance use as a coping mechanism.

   - ○ <u>Coping Tools</u>: Develop healthy coping mechanisms, such as journaling or engaging in hobbies.

   - ○ <u>Acceptance and Commitment Therapy (ACT)</u>: Techniques from ACT can be incredibly valuable. ACT teaches us to accept what we can't control and commit to actions that enrich our lives. In your situation, this means accepting the reality of your loved one's health while focusing on providing the best care you can.

   - ○ <u>Mindfulness meditation</u>: It helps you stay present with your emotions, acknowledging feelings of sadness or grief without letting them overwhelm you or drive you towards substance use. (Check out doctorolson.com/media for guided meditations.)

   - ○ <u>Cognitive-Behavioral Therapy (CBT)</u>: Excellent for tackling those negative thoughts that might creep in. When you find yourself thinking, "I can't handle this," try to reframe it to, "I can handle this one day at a time." It's about challenging and changing those automatic negative thoughts into something more manageable.

- Gratitude: Don't underestimate the power of gratitude. It's strongly supported by research as a key to boosting wellbeing. Keeping a gratitude journal helps you focus on the positive aspects, even in tough times. It could be something as simple as appreciating a moment of connection with your loved one or learning something new through your caregiving experience.

5. **Neglect of Self-Care**: Caregivers often prioritize the needs of the person they are caring for above their own, leading to neglect of their physical and mental health needs, which are essential for addiction recovery.

- Set aside regular time for self-care activities, treating them as essential.

- Regularly assess and attend to your own health needs.

6. **Difficulty Maintaining Routine**: The unpredictable nature of caregiving can disrupt routines, making it difficult for recovering individuals to maintain a structured schedule that supports their recovery process.

- Identify and prioritize the most critical aspects of your recovery routine.

o Use the strategies below to infuse some flexibility into your routine, making it more adaptable to the unpredictable nature of caregiving:

    i.   <u>Build in Buffer Time</u>: Allow extra time between activities to accommodate unexpected delays or emergencies. This buffer can help reduce stress when things don't go as planned.

    ii.   <u>Create Daily Themes</u>: Instead of a rigid hour-by-hour schedule, consider having daily themes or focuses–like medication management (sorting and stocking) on one day, and doctors' appointments on another. This approach provides structure while allowing flexibility within each day.

    iii.   <u>Develop Routines for Unpredictable Tasks</u>: For tasks that are unpredictable in timing (like dealing with sudden health issues), have a predefined set of steps or a checklist to follow. This can make managing these tasks more efficient.

    iv.   <u>Use Technology</u>: Leverage technology like smartphone apps for reminders, scheduling, and tracking important tasks. This can help in organizing and reshuffling tasks quickly. (See Technology section on page 184.)

7. **Reduced Access to Treatment and Support Services**: Caregivers may find it hard to access treatment and support services due to caregiving duties, geographical isolation, or financial constraints.

   o Investigate local resources and services that offer flexibility, such as home-based therapy or online support groups. Some groups even offer services similar to childcare, but for adult dependents, while your group is in session. Check with a local senior center or larger institutes with specialists.

   o Discuss with healthcare providers about integrating recovery needs into the caregiving plan.

8. **Risk of Codependency**: In some cases, the caregiver-patient relationship can evolve into a codependent dynamic, which can be detrimental to the recovery process of a person with a history of addiction. Understanding codependency can be pivotal, especially for individuals in caregiving roles or those dealing with addiction.

   Codependency is a relationship dynamic wherein an individual excessively relies on the needs and behaviors of others to dictate their own behaviors and emotions, often at the expense of their own needs and well-being. It frequently develops in relationships where one person is struggling with addiction or illness. Codependency often originates in childhood, typically in families where there is addiction, chronic illness, or emotional dysfunction. Children in these families may learn to suppress their own needs in an effort to take care of a parent or sibling. Codependency can also develop in the relationship between a caregiver with addiction issues and a care recipient through a complex interplay of emotional and behavioral patterns.

Here are some aspects of how it might unfold:

- ○ <u>Caregiver's Emotional Dependency</u>: The caregiver with addiction issues may become emotionally dependent on (to an imbalanced/unhealthy degree) the care recipient for validation, self-esteem, and a sense of purpose. This dependency may stem from feelings of guilt or inadequacy associated with their addiction, or something else.

- ○ <u>Enabling Behaviors</u>: The care recipient, in turn, might enable the caregiver's addictive behavior, either consciously or unconsciously. They might downplay symptoms or provide money or medications out of feelings of gratitude or obligation. This could be due to fear of losing the caregiver's support, a desire to avoid conflict, or a misunderstanding of how to help the caregiver with their addiction.

- ○ <u>Reversal of Roles</u>: In some cases, the care recipient might start taking on the role of the caregiver, trying to manage or cover up issues related to the caregiver's addiction. This role reversal can lead to a codepenent dynamic where the care recipient feels *responsible* for the caregiver's well-being (note: this is beyond simple human compassion).

- <u>Fear of Abandonment</u>: The caregiver may fear losing the relationship if they confront their addiction or change the dynamics. Similarly, the care recipient may fear being left without care or support, leading to a situation where both parties avoid addressing the issues.

- <u>Neglect of Personal Needs</u>: The above point can lead to neglect. The caregiver, focused on their addiction and caregiving duties, might neglect their own health and emotional needs. The care recipient, in turn, may neglect their own needs to avoid upsetting the status quo.

- <u>Shared Denial</u>: Both parties might engage in a shared denial about the severity of the caregiver's addiction and its impact on their relationship and caregiving duties. This denial reinforces the codependent behavior, as neither party is willing to acknowledge and address the core issues.

- <u>Guilt and Obligation</u>: The caregiver might feel guilty about their addiction and compensate by overextending themselves in caregiving duties. The care recipient might feel obligated to tolerate or support the caregiver's addiction because of the care they receive.

- Dependency for Self-Worth: The caregiver's sense of self-worth may become heavily reliant on their role as a caregiver, intertwining their identity with both their addiction and their caregiving responsibilities.

- Lack of Boundaries: There may be a lack of healthy boundaries, with the caregiver possibly overstepping or neglecting their own well-being for the sake of caregiving, while the care recipient becomes increasingly reliant on the caregiver's presence and support.

- Mutual Avoidance of Change: Both the caregiver and the care recipient might avoid making changes, even if those changes are necessary for the caregiver's recovery and the overall health of the relationship.

In such a relationship, the intertwined issues of addiction and caregiving can create a codependent dynamic where both parties struggle to maintain a healthy and functional relationship. Codependency can lead to mental health issues, such as anxiety, depression, and stress. It can also result in neglect of one's own health, needs, and well-being. Recognizing and addressing this codependency is crucial for the well-being of both the caregiver and the care recipient.

Professional help, such as therapy or counseling, can be instrumental in breaking these patterns and establishing healthier relationship dynamics. Codependency is a learned behavior, which means it can be unlearned through therapy and personal growth efforts. One book, <u>The Betrayal Bond: Breaking Free of Exploitive Relationships</u> by Patrick Carnes, Ph.D., is a resource for growing out of codependency. Support groups like Codependents Anonymous (CoDA) can also be beneficial.

Overcoming codependency involves:

- <u>Learning to establish healthy boundaries</u>: Develop a strong sense of self, and engage in open and honest communication.

- <u>Practicing being alone</u>: Spend time alone to get comfortable with your own company. Notice how being without the opinions of others can feel freeing, even if a little adrift. Discover a new hobby or book. This can help reduce the fear of abandonment or loneliness that often fuels codependency. It can also increase enjoyment of yourself and increase self-esteem.

- <u>Identifying & Challenging codependent thoughts</u>: Such thoughts may sound like, "I have to keep them happy, or everything will fall apart," or "If they're unhappy, it must be my fault, and I need to fix it," or "I shouldn't say no, or they might not love or need me anymore."

When you recognize a codependent thought or behavior, challenge it. Ask yourself if there's a healthier way to view the situation or respond. Consider the following responses to a codependent thought:

i. "Their feelings are their responsibility, not mine. I can offer support, but I can't control their emotions or choices."

ii. "It's okay for someone to feel unhappy sometimes; I don't need to fix everything for them."

- Practicing saying no: Being able to say no is crucial in overcoming codependency. Start small and gradually build up your confidence in refusing requests that make you uncomfortable or are unreasonable. You could start by role playing with a trusted person about how you might say no to a request, then find opportunities to do so in real life, like declining a paper handout from a stranger. Work up to "bigger nos," like asking someone to wait while you finish a task or declining an invitation with a simple "no, thanks" in favor of time alone.

- Prioritizing self-care: Learn to recognize and meet one's own needs and desires. Discover your own cues for when you are tired, need a snack, need more/less social connection, or time to think. Pause occasionally throughout the day to check in on your physical sensations (e.g., hunger pangs) and mood shifts (e.g., irritability), then try out possible solutions, like having a snack or putting on some good music.

Recognizing and addressing codependency is essential for the health and well-being of both parties in a relationship. It can lead to less anxiety, better communication, and lead to healthier choices for yourself. It's especially important for caregivers and those in recovery from addiction to be aware of these dynamics to foster healthier relationships and personal well-being, as there are so many opportunities for creating an imbalance in met needs.

Relapse and Caregiving

1. **Plan for Relapse Prevention**: Recognize triggers and have a plan in place to prevent relapse. This includes strategies for dealing with stress and temptation. There are many resources geared towards relapse prevention efforts, so we'll leave the details there, but know that relapse prevention is also a part of navigating the role of caregiver.

2. **Recovering from Relapse**: Recovering from a relapse while managing caregiving duties involves a step-by-step process that starts with acknowledging the relapse without self-blame. Caregiving often adds layers of stress, so it's crucial to reach out to your support

system—whether that's a therapist, support group, or trusted friend—to ensure you're not navigating recovery alone.

Next, assess the circumstances that led to the relapse by identifying triggers. These could stem from caregiving-related stressors, like exhaustion, feelings of isolation, or emotional strain, or from external factors like social or environmental challenges. Reflecting on these triggers can help you adjust your coping strategies, such as setting boundaries or seeking additional caregiving resources, to manage similar situations in the future. Reinforce your recovery plan by re-engaging with treatment options, like therapy, meetings, or group support, and consider incorporating new tools tailored to your role as a caregiver, such as mindfulness exercises or stress management techniques you can do during short breaks.

Lastly, practice self-compassion. Relapse is a common part of recovery, and being a caregiver doesn't mean you have to be perfect. Acknowledge the effort you're putting into both your recovery and caregiving, and take things one step at a time. Each day is an opportunity to move forward.

3. **Delegate Caregiving Tasks**: If you're in the midst of a relapse or freshly out of one, delegate tasks to other family members or professional caregivers to reduce stress and focus on recovery. Delegating caregiving tasks

can be particularly challenging for someone struggling with addiction for several reasons.

Why is Delegating Difficult?

A caregiver struggling with addiction might hesitate to delegate tasks because their addiction often amplifies feelings of guilt, shame, and responsibility. Addressing these challenges involves a delicate balance of recognizing one's limits, seeking appropriate help, and ensuring the best care for their loved ones. Consider the following points and work through them (likely with the help of a therapist) to make delegating something you look forward to and use whenever possible to make life easier. If you are someone supporting a caregiver with addiction issues, see if any of the below points offer a way to support them better in their caregiving efforts:

➤ <u>Trust Issues and Control</u>: Individuals with addiction often struggle with trust issues, stemming from their personal battles. They might find it hard to believe that someone else can provide the same level of care or attention to their loved one. This lack of trust can make it difficult to relinquish control and delegate tasks.

➤ <u>Guilt and Shame</u>: People with addiction may already feel guilty or ashamed about their condition. Admitting they need help with caregiving can exacerbate these feelings, as it might be perceived as an admission of their inability to manage their responsibilities.

➤ <u>Fear of Judgment</u>: There can be a fear of being judged or stigmatized by others if they disclose their addiction issues. This fear might deter them from seeking help or sharing caregiving responsibilities, as it could expose their struggles to family members, friends, or professional caregivers.

➤ <u>Denial of Addiction Severity</u>: Sometimes, individuals may be in denial about the severity of their addiction and how it impacts their caregiving abilities. This denial can prevent them from recognizing the need to delegate tasks.

➤ <u>Personal Pride and Identity</u>: For some, the role of caregiver becomes a core part of their identity. Admitting that they need help and delegating tasks can feel like a loss of purpose or personal failure, which is particularly difficult for those already struggling with the low self-esteem often associated with addiction.

➤ <u>Impact on Recovery Efforts</u>: Engaging in caregiving can be a form of coping or distraction from addiction. Handing over caregiving responsibilities might leave the individual with more free time, which they fear could lead to increased substance use or relapse if not managed properly.

➤ <u>Logistical Challenges</u>: Finding reliable help can be difficult, especially if the caregiver's addiction has led to a constrained financial situation or a limited social network. The process of identifying, hiring, and training someone else can be overwhelming.

➤ <u>Concerns about Consistency in Care</u>: Caregivers in general may be concerned about maintaining a consistent care routine if tasks are delegated. They might worry that new caregivers will not be aware of specific needs or preferences of the care recipient.

➤ <u>Worry about the Care Recipient's Reaction</u>: They may fear that asking others to step in could upset the care recipient, who might be used to their care routine or feel uneasy about changes. The caregiver might also fear that the care recipient will feel abandoned or resentful, which can trigger the caregiver's own feelings of inadequacy or failure tied to their addiction. This emotional cycle can make it even harder for them to ask for help, despite knowing that delegating tasks could provide the space and support they need for their recovery. The addiction's influence often deepens their reluctance,

> as it reinforces a sense of obligation to overcompensate and hide their struggles.

Other Helpful Strategies

1. **Maintain Open Communication**: Be honest with family members and the care recipient about the challenges and progress in dealing with addiction. This might mean having a personal or group check-in day wherein you review how the last week, for example, has gone and if there are any supports that worked well, that need to be put in place, or need troubleshooting.

2. **Monitor Medication and Substance Access**: If the addiction involves substances, caregivers should be cautious about access to medication and other substances in the caregiving environment. This might mean you have accountability to someone who knows you have access; this accountability might simply be regular check ins, or it might be more rigorous. Consider having a backup plan for times when being near such medication would prove trying, such as an automated dispensing system or a neighbor/friend that can take over for the day while you attend to your recovery needs. In the end, managing medication might simply not be in your best interest, and instead you will need to find a more permanent solution that doesn't involve you having close access to medication.

3. **Keep Regular Appointments**: Adhere to regular appointments with healthcare providers, both for addiction treatment and caregiving support.

4. **Document Progress**: Keeping a journal or log of progress in both caregiving and addiction recovery can provide a sense of accomplishment and a tool for reflection. Keeping a journal or log of progress in both caregiving and addiction recovery can be highly beneficial for several reasons:

   o Tracking Progress: A journal provides a tangible way to track progress over time. Seeing improvements, even small ones, can be motivating and affirming. It also helps in identifying patterns or triggers in both caregiving challenges and addiction recovery.

   o Emotional Release: Writing about experiences and feelings can be a therapeutic form of emotional release. It allows for the expression of thoughts and emotions that might be difficult to articulate verbally.

   o Enhancing Self-Awareness: Journaling encourages self-reflection, leading to greater self-awareness. Understanding your emotional responses, stressors, and coping mechanisms can be crucial in both caregiving and managing addiction.

   o Problem-Solving: Journaling can aid in problem-solving by allowing you to work through challenges on paper. Writing down problems and potential solutions can provide clarity and perspective.

- Identifying Patterns: Regular entries can help in identifying patterns related to addiction triggers or caregiving stressors. Recognizing these patterns is the first step in developing strategies to manage them effectively.

- Setting and Reviewing Goals: A journal can be used to set short-term and long-term goals in caregiving and recovery. Regularly reviewing and adjusting these goals can keep you focused and on track.

- Reducing Stress: The act of writing can be a stress-relieving activity. It offers a quiet, introspective time to unwind and reflect, which is especially beneficial for caregivers who often operate in high-stress environments.

- Documenting Successes and Challenges: Keeping a record of successes boosts confidence and provides a sense of accomplishment. Similarly, documenting challenges can be instructive for understanding areas that need more attention or different strategies.

- A Source for Future Reflection: Looking back on previous journal entries can provide valuable insights into your journey, showing how far you've come and what you've learned. It can also be a source of encouragement during difficult times.

- Communication Tool: Sometimes, journal entries can be a useful tool to communicate with therapists, counselors, or support groups. They provide a concrete way to share your experiences and get targeted feedback.

- o <u>Personal Accountability</u>: Regular journaling fosters a sense of personal accountability. It serves as a reminder of your commitments to your caregiving duties and your recovery journey.

In essence, journaling is a versatile tool that serves multiple purposes in both caregiving and addiction recovery. It supports emotional health, aids in tracking progress and setbacks, and assists in personal growth and understanding.

For People Supporting Caregivers with Addiction

Caring for a loved one is a demanding task, and when the caregiver faces addiction issues, the complexities multiply. This is also true for the families supporting a caregiver who is struggling with addiction. Whether you're near or far, understanding the dynamics at play, recognizing the signs of trouble, and knowing how to effectively intervene can make a significant difference. Here, we'll review practical strategies and compassionate approaches to support your loved one in their dual role as a caregiver and someone contending with addiction. We'll also discuss how to ensure the safety and well-being of the care recipient, maintain healthy family dynamics, and provide the necessary support to the caregiver on their path to recovery and effective caregiving.

1. **Recognize Signs of Addiction and Codependency**:
   The first signs of someone struggling with addiction may not necessarily be observing them use or have drugs in their possession. Instead, some signs that may help to be aware of include neglecting responsibilities and changes in behavior). Additionally, it can be helpful to look for signs of codependency, as this often accompanies addiction and can further complicate the dynamics between everyone involved. These signs may include sacrificing one's own needs for the addict and enabling their addictive behaviors. Example: If the caregiver frequently misses medication times due to substance use or if family members constantly cover up for the caregiver's absences or mistakes, these could be signs to watch for.

2. **Open Communication:** As tough as it may sound, being open about your concerns, if said kindly, is the best option for looking out for all involved. If being proactive, validate that this is just a precaution given past issues and that you appreciate their dedication to both the care recipient and their own recovery. Talk individually or hold a small family meeting to discuss concerns about the caregiver's addiction and its impact on caregiving. Approach this conversation with empathy, focusing on how the addiction affects everyone, including the caregiver. Example: "We've noticed these specific changes and are worried about how this is affecting you and Mom's care." This may be best done in the presence

of a mental health professional who specializes in addiction issues.

3. **Set Healthy Boundaries:** Clearly define what behaviors the family will not tolerate and the consequences. Example: "If we find that you're under the influence while caregiving, we'll need to arrange for alternative care for Dad during those times."

4. **Encourage Professional Help**: Offer resources for addiction treatment, such as contact information for local support groups or rehabilitation centers. Example: "We found this support group that could help you, and we're willing to go with you to the first meeting."

5. **Provide Support**: Show compassion and understanding. Let them know their worth beyond their addiction. There is often shame and secrecy associated with addiction. Thus, it is important to approach the conversation with compassion and care rather than from a place of judgments and blame. Example: "We know this is hard for you, and we're here to support you, not just as a caregiver but as a person who deserves help and care."

6. **Create a Caregiving Plan**: Discuss and document a plan that includes contingencies in case the caregiver is unable to fulfill their duties. Example: "Let's create a schedule where other family members can step in or explore part-time professional care options."

7. **Monitor the Care Recipient's Well-being**: Regularly check-in with the family member being cared for to

ensure their needs are being met. Example: Setting up weekly visits or calls to assess the care recipient's condition and their comfort level with the caregiving situation.

8. **Educate About Codependency**: Encourage the caregiver to explore literature or online resources about codependency (e.g., SAMHSA.gov). Example: Providing books or articles that explain how codependency works and its effects on relationships.

9. **Self-Care for Family Members**: Engage in activities that reduce stress and provide emotional relief. Example: Family members might join a support group for relatives of addicts, take up a relaxing hobby, or schedule regular therapy sessions.

10. **Seek External Support**: Consider consulting with a therapist or counselor who specializes in addiction and family dynamics.

11. **Plan for Relapse**: Acknowledge that relapse can be part of the recovery journey and have a plan to handle it. That may be seeking additional professional support or another caregiving arrangement to ensure safety and care quality. Remember that a relapse does not mean failure, it may just be a detour on the road to recovery.

Implementing these strategies can help a family navigate a caregiving situation involving addiction, ensuring the well-being of both the caregiver and the care recipient.

Support at a Distance

More than 1 in 10 informal family caregivers live at least two hours away from the loved one they care for (AARP, April 2019). When family members don't live nearby but need to address issues related to a caregiver with addiction who is caring for a family member, they can still take effective actions, albeit remotely. Here are ways to adapt the strategies for long-distance family involvement:

1. <u>Virtual Check-ins and Communication</u>: Regular video calls or phone check-ins with both the caregiver and the care recipient can help monitor the situation. For example, weekly video chats can provide visual cues on the caregiver's and care recipient's well-being.

2. <u>Coordinate with Local Resources</u>: Research and coordinate with local resources like home healthcare services, addiction support groups, and social services in the caregiver's area. For instance, you can arrange for a local home health aide to assist periodically, providing relief and oversight.

3. <u>Remote Monitoring Technologies</u>: If all people involved are agreeable, utilize technology for remote monitoring, like installing cameras or medical alert systems, to keep an eye on the care recipient's safety.

4. <u>Enlist Friends or Professionals</u>: If there are friends, neighbors, or community members nearby, ask if they can periodically check in or provide updates. Or, schedule regular assessments by healthcare

professionals to evaluate the care recipient's health and the quality of care being provided.

5. <u>Remote Education and Support</u>: Send the caregiver informational resources on addiction and caregiving. Encourage them to join online support groups where they can get advice and support.

6. <u>Financial and Administrative Assistance</u>: Offer to help with administrative tasks or financial management remotely, which can alleviate some of the caregiver's burdens.

7. <u>Develop an Emergency Plan</u>: Have a plan in place for emergencies, including local contacts, emergency services, and a process for intervening if the situation becomes critical.

8. <u>Hire a Care Manager</u>: Consider hiring a geriatric care manager or a similar professional who can oversee the care recipient's situation and provide regular updates.

9. <u>Legal and Financial Planning</u>: Engage in legal and financial planning to ensure the care recipient's needs are met, even from afar. This might include setting up a power of attorney, a healthcare proxy, or a care fund.

Conclusion

Caregiving while experiencing addiction means taking on a meaningful challenge for another amidst a personal challenge within. It requires a balance of fulfilling caregiving responsibilities while actively engaging in addiction treatment and self-care. Remember, recovery is a continuous process, relapses are often part of this process, and seeking help is a sign of strength, not weakness. Through perseverance and support, caregivers can offer quality care while working towards their own recovery and well-being.

Personality Among Caregivers

> *"There are only four kinds of people in the world - those who have been caregivers, those who are currently caregivers, those who will be caregivers, and those who will need caregivers."*
> - U.S. First Lady Rosalynn Carter

Caregiving draws on the most intimate aspects of our personalities. Close quarters can amplify these personality traits, for better or for worse. This is especially relevant considering the majority of care recipients who are not living in a facility live *with* a caregiver (AARP 2020). Personality can be thought of as the interplay of thought patterns, behaviors, and interpersonal dynamics. For the purpose of this chapter, we will discuss personality in terms of those enduring behaviors that we often feel "define us" as individuals, that we engage in across contexts and time. This can include behaviors like repeatedly choosing experiences that offer predictability over spontaneity, or being considered optimistic because you generally see the positive side of situations. Personality is not a fleeting mood or temporary emotion, like feeling angry after a specific incident. Unlike personality, moods and emotions are short-lived and can change rapidly depending on circumstances.

Personality is the broader pattern of behaviors, thoughts, and emotions that characterize an individual over time, while traits are specific characteristics that make up this pattern. Traits, such as openness or extraversion, are the building blocks of personality, contributing to its overall expression.

We will focus more on traits of the everyday caregiver, rather than personality disorders. However, some traits, when taken to extremes can cause significant distress and dysfunction, to the point of being considered a disorder.

Personality influences if an individual takes on caregiving itself, and how a caregiver approaches challenges, communicates with their care recipient, and values the act of caregiving. While some caregivers may possess seemingly boundless empathy, others may grapple with personality traits that complicate their caregiving journey. Impatience can strain relationships, introversion may lead to feelings of overstimulation, and perfectionism can breed burnout. A caregiver's unique traits can serve as both assets and liabilities, shaping not only their approach to caregiving but also their emotional well-being.

An Introverted Caregiver's Story

Meet Daniel, an introverted caregiver who often sought the gentle hum of solitude. His caregiving story unfolded against the backdrop of his introverted temperament, a canvas where solitude wasn't a void but a serene lake where his thoughts gently rippled.

In those days, Daniel's life was quiet, marked by the soft cadence of his spouse's needs. As an introvert, he thrived in those hushed moments of care, where words often remained unspoken but feelings were deeply understood. The solitude, instead of isolation, was a sanctuary where he could give without reserve, finding solace in the exchange of glances, the warmth of a touch, and the silent understanding between them.

But as his spouse's health declined, Daniel's life was thrown into turmoil. The demands of constant medical appointments, coordinating treatments, and frequent interactions with healthcare professionals left him overwhelmed and drained. He could no longer find refuge in the solitude he once treasured; instead, he felt trapped in a cycle of noise and demands that left him anxious and irritable. He grew distant, realizing that his own health and spirit were fraying under the strain.

One day, after an especially exhausting week, Daniel hit a breaking point when he heard his unusually impatient and harsh tone with one of the clinical staff. He recognized he couldn't keep going like this. He needed space to recharge and reconnect with himself if he was going to be a supportive caregiver. He began setting small routines—moments to read, walk outside, or simply breathe in quiet places. With time, he learned to express his need for solitude to friends and family, who offered support and respite. These breaks became his refuge, allowing him to return with renewed patience and empathy.

Gradually, Daniel found a new rhythm, balancing his need for quiet with the demands of caregiving. Though challenges remained, he nurtured his introverted soul by building moments of peace into his days. With creativity and the understanding of loved ones, he managed to honor both his caregiving role and his need for solitude, becoming a steady, compassionate anchor for his spouse.

One Approach to Personality

There are a variety of approaches out there that are used to define, value, and measure personality. We'll keep it relatively simple here and break it down using one common approach. Developed through the work of several researchers over decades, the "OCEAN" acronym refers to a specific grouping of traits that defines personality. According to this model, personality is broken down into five specific domains, which is why it is often called the Big Five personality traits, a widely respected model in psychology for describing human personality. The Big Five traits are Openness, Conscientiousness, Extraversion, Agreeableness, and Neuroticism. Each trait represents a spectrum, and an individual's personality is described based on where they fall on each of five spectrums. Research so far has uncovered some interesting insights into how personality can interact with caregiving, but there is still much more to explore. Let's take a brief look at each trait of the Big Five model:

Openness: This trait features characteristics such as imagination, insight, and a wide range of interests. People high in openness are often curious, creative, and open to new experiences and ideas. They tend to enjoy art, adventure, and unusual ideas. Conversely, those low in openness may prefer familiarity and routine, and are more conservative in their thinking and behavior.

Conscientiousness: Conscientiousness includes high levels of thoughtfulness, impulse control, and goal-directed behaviors. Highly conscientious people are organized, mindful of details, and responsible. They plan ahead and are diligent. Those with lower conscientiousness might be more spontaneous, less focused on details, and more likely to procrastinate.

Extraversion: Extraversion is characterized by excitability, sociability, talkativeness, assertiveness, and high amounts of emotional expressiveness. Extroverts gain energy from social interaction and are often enthusiastic and action-oriented. Introverts, or those lower in extraversion, may prefer solitude, be more reserved, and expend energy in social situations.

Agreeableness: This trait reflects attributes such as trust, altruism, kindness, affection, and other prosocial behaviors. People who score high in agreeableness are often cooperative, warm, and considerate. Those lower in this trait might be more competitive, sometimes confrontational, and more likely to put their interests above others.

Neuroticism: Neuroticism includes traits such as moodiness, sadness, and emotional instability. Individuals who score high in neuroticism often experience emotional instability, anxiety, irritability, and sadness. On the flip side, they also tend to be more vigilant, self-aware, and cautious. Those with lower scores in neuroticism tend to be more emotionally stable and resilient.

It's important to note that these traits are not definitive boxes that people fit into but rather spectrums that describe tendencies in behavior and personality. Positions on the spectrum can change over time and be influenced by external factors. The Big Five ("OCEAN") model is valued for its scientific backing and is considered a robust framework for understanding personality.

To learn more about your own personality traits, the best option is a formal personality test by a trained psychologist. However, those can take more steps to arrange than most people are up for. One alternative is to check out a free online questionnaire by doing a search for "Five Factor Personality test" or "Big Five Personality test." Keep in mind the quality varies widely in terms of accuracy of results; in your search, select one from a reputable source, such as a well-established university or organization.

Where Did My Personality Go?

Many caregivers perceive a shift in their personality after caregiving for a while. When feeling stressed or overwhelmed, it can feel like you're a different you—and we don't always like the new version. Sometimes it feels like a disappearance altogether of certain traits. Your typical concerns or preferences take the backseat to the needs of the care recipient, such that your behavior reflects a whole new set of priorities. Additionally, there is often too little time while caregiving to process ambiguous losses–where there is not a complete/apparent loss, but instead a partial/invisible loss—and these losses build up: loss of identity, lost libido, loss of freedom, and financial losses, to name a few. This can lead to a feeling of being in identity limbo, where you're still outwardly you, but everything feels different. Other shifts in behavior can occur, such as having identified as an extrovert, yet the isolation so common to caregiving atrophies social skills or perhaps you are so tired from the day's responsibilities that your pre-caregiving social schedule seems more like a chore than a recharge. For this reason, you may wonder if you're "still an extrovert" or which personality aspects to identify with. If you've been caregiving a while, think back to times prior to caregiving and the more enduring traits across your lifespan. These are likely to be more fundamental to who you are. In turn, these fundamental traits are likely to point to experiences that are most satisfying to your core self.

Traits Among Caregivers

To date, few studies have examined the influence of personality traits on the caregiving experience (e.g., Baharudin et al., 2019; Luchetti et al, 2021; Hajek & König, 2018). What's been discovered is that caregivers select caregiving strategies based on their own personality (Melo et al., 2017), and that caregivers may benefit from therapeutic interventions tailored to their individual personality profile (Löckenhoff et al., 2011). Given we are in the early stages of understanding personality's impact on caregiving, it seemed helpful to offer ideas in the following sections that are based on my personal and professional experiences. I'll also make use of the more general understanding of personality (outside of the caregiving context). With that in mind, let's consider the ways in which personality may impact the various facets of caregiving.

Below we examine each of the Big Five personality traits, focusing on the extremes of each trait (high and low) in the context of caregiving.

Openness

High Openness

Individuals with high levels of openness in caregiving are often creative, open to new ideas, and willing to try innovative approaches in care. They may explore unconventional therapies, seek out diverse resources, and introduce varied activities for the care recipient. Higher levels of openness relate to more positive perceptions of the caregiving relationship and caregiving-related growth (Hollis-Sawyer, 2003).

Challenges of those with high levels of openness may include a tendency to constantly seek new methods, which can lead to inconsistency in care. There's also a risk of overlooking established, effective routines in pursuit of novelty.

- o *Interpersonal Communication*: Caregivers with high openness might enthusiastically propose numerous new ideas or alternative therapies, which can overwhelm family members, healthcare providers, or the care recipient. Before introducing a new concept or treatment option, prioritize and research thoroughly. Present only one or two well-considered ideas at a time during discussions to avoid overwhelming others.

○ *Task Management*: Balance your innovative ideas with practicality. Ensure that essential routines are maintained even as you explore new caregiving methods. A tendency to frequently change care routines or try new methods may lead to inconsistency in care, which can be unsettling for the care recipient. Implement a 'trial and evaluation' approach. Introduce one new method or change at a time, stick with it for an agreed period, then evaluate its effectiveness before making further changes.

○ *Emotional Well-being*: High openness can sometimes lead to overstimulation or distraction, as the caregiver may pursue many different interests or ideas simultaneously. Schedule specific times for exploring new interests or hobbies, ensuring that there is ample time to experience the peace of no proposed changes. Balance your need for intellectual stimulation with periods of focused, routine care.

○ *Meaning-Making*: Individuals with high openness may sometimes find the routine aspects of caregiving to be monotonous and lacking intellectual stimulation, which can impact their sense of fulfillment. To find meaning in caregiving, focus on the creative and innovative aspects it can offer. For instance, you could document the caregiving journey through a blog or a photo project. This not only serves as a creative outlet but also helps in appreciating the unique moments and lessons learned through caregiving. Additionally, consider exploring new ways of connecting with the care recipient, such as engaging in thoughtful conversations about their life experiences or reading and discussing books together. These activities can provide intellectual stimulation and deepen the emotional bond, adding a layer of richness and purpose to the caregiving experience.

Low Openness

Caregivers with low openness typically prefer familiar routines and traditional methods of care. They value consistency and may be more comfortable sticking to established caregiving practices.

However, they might struggle with adapting to changes in the care recipient's needs or be resistant to new but potentially beneficial caregiving strategies.

- *Interpersonal Communication*: Caregivers with low openness may be resistant to discussing or considering new caregiving approaches, which can lead to conflicts with family members or healthcare providers offering different methods. Practice active listening when someone proposes new ideas. Even if initially resistant, acknowledge their suggestions and agree to research or discuss them further with healthcare professionals. This approach shows openness to dialogue and helps in making informed decisions.

- o *Task Management:* A tendency to stick to familiar routines might make it challenging to adapt to the evolving needs of the care recipient. Start by introducing small changes that can improve care. For example, if suggested to alter the dietary plan of the care recipient, try incorporating one new recipe a week. This gradual approach helps in slowly adapting to necessary changes without feeling overwhelmed. Another consideration is willingness to entertain certain treatment choices, such as a DNR (do not resuscitate) order, if that conflicts with your own beliefs. When treatment options are difficult to go along with, seek input from healthcare providers or listen to the reasoning of others who find themselves in a similar situation. It can make mutual understanding easier.

- o *Emotional Well-being:* Being less open to new experiences can sometimes lead to feelings of isolation or monotony in the caregiving role. Establish a small, consistent change in your routine that brings joy or relaxation, like a weekly hobby or outdoor activity. This can provide a refreshing break from the caregiving routine while maintaining a sense of predictability.

- o *Meaning-Making:* To find meaning in caregiving, focus on the stability and comfort your consistency brings to the care recipient. For instance, create a memory book or timeline that chronicles the caregiving journey, highlighting the moments of joy, challenges overcome, and the positive impact of your care. This can help you see the value in the routine and reliability you provide.

Conscientiousness

High Conscientiousness

A caregiver's level of conscientiousness relates to their use of healthy strategies to handle stress or difficult emotions (Hooker, Frazier, & Monahan, 1994), as well as experiencing better mental and physical health (Löckenhoff et al., 2011). Highly conscientious caregivers are organized, reliable, and diligent. They excel in managing schedules, medication, and planning care-related tasks efficiently.

The downside is a potential for rigidity, where they may become overly critical or stressed if plans go awry. They might also struggle with flexibility, which is often required in dynamic caregiving situations.

- *Interpersonal Communication*: Highly conscientious caregivers might focus too much on efficiency and details, potentially overlooking the emotional aspects of communication. Actively practice empathy during conversations. For instance, when discussing care plans, consciously ask the care recipient about their feelings and preferences, not just their physical needs.

- *Task Management*: A strong focus on organization and planning can lead to rigidity, making it hard to adapt to unexpected changes. Create a flexible care schedule that allows for unforeseen events. For example, while having a daily routine, allocate some 'buffer time' each day for unplanned needs or activities.

- *Emotional Well-being:* High conscientiousness can lead to self-criticism or stress when things don't go as planned. Practice self-compassion exercises. Remind yourself that caregiving is unpredictable and it's okay to not always have everything under control. One self-critical belief of highly conscientious individuals relates to their beliefs about illness: "I feel like my loved one's illness is something I should be able to fix, and if I can't, I'm failing." While we know logically we can't fix it, there sometimes persists an emotional desire to do so. Acknowledging that desire can be a balm in itself. Also consider scheduling regular relaxation activities like yoga or meditation to manage stress.

- *Meaning-Making:* The tendency to focus on tasks might overshadow the more profound, emotional rewards of caregiving. At the end of each day, reflect on and write down moments of connection or gratitude experienced, not just tasks completed. Jot down just a few words or write more at length, either is helpful. This helps in recognizing the deeper value and impact of your caregiving beyond the checklist.

Low Conscientiousness

Those lower in conscientiousness may bring a more flexible and spontaneous approach to caregiving, which can sometimes be beneficial in adapting to the unexpected.

However, they may face challenges with organization and consistency, possibly neglecting important tasks or struggling to maintain a structured caregiving routine.

- o *Interpersonal Communication:* Caregivers with lower conscientiousness might be less structured in communication, leading to missed information or misunderstandings. Use tools like written notes or digital reminders to keep track of important points discussed in family meetings or with healthcare providers. Additionally, develop a habit of regular check-ins with family members or healthcare providers to stay on track.

- o *Task Management:* A more relaxed approach to tasks can result in inconsistency in caregiving routines. Implement simple organizational systems, like a basic daily checklist for medication and meals, to ensure consistency in care without it being overwhelming. Additionally, ensure that more comprehensive plans, like DNR or other healthcare directives, are outlined in writing to prevent future misunderstanding and headache.

- o *Emotional Well-being:* Caregivers with lower conscientiousness might overlook their own need for structure, which can affect emotional stability. Establish a simple but consistent self-care routine, such as morning walks or regular brief catch-ups with friends, to bring a sense of order and personal well-being.

- o *Meaning-Making:* A laid-back nature might lead to a lack of recognition of the significance of their role in caregiving. When possible, regularly engage in conversations with the care recipient about how your care is impacting their life. Hearing appreciation or understanding their improved quality of life can reinforce the importance of your role. See some prompts for this discussion in the Versatile Strategies section on page 166.

Extraversion

High Extraversion

Extraverted caregivers often bring energy and positive social interactions to their caregiving role. They are usually good communicators and may find it easier to coordinate with healthcare providers and involve the care recipient in social activities. Caregivers implement a range of approaches to bring out the desired behavior of care recipients; extroverted caregivers were found to be less confrontational, when considering approaches such as avoiding conflict, reassuring, distracting, and being restrictive (Melo et al., 2017).

The challenges for extroverts can involve difficulty with alone time and a tendency to overextend themselves in caregiving and other social commitments.

- *Interpersonal Communication:* Engage in social activities with the care recipient, but also respect their need for quiet times. An extroverted caregiver might organize video calls with friends or family to share updates, balanced out by parallel or quiet activities, such as each person drawing or puzzle time together. This allows them to engage actively with others but gives downtime.

o   *Task Management:* Delegate tasks that require solitude or focused attention if they are draining for you. Take the lead in organizing social activities for the care recipient, such as planning visits with friends or arranging group outings. This plays to the extroverted caregiver's strengths in social coordination and provides them with the interaction they thrive on. If the caregiver has friends who are also caregivers - or friends who simply need to complete the same task – the caregiver can try doing errands together. This allows for task completion, while filling the social cup, and while not requiring extra time to be carved out in the schedule to do so. For example, instead of making dinner alone for only the caregiver and the care recipient, the caregiver and their friend can make the meal together for themselves and both of their care recipients and then enjoy the meal together as well. If the caregiver does not currently have friends who fit this description, this may be a great time to think about joining a caregiver's support group (search 'caregiver support group for [condition]' online or talk with your health care provider).

o   *Emotional Well-being:* Participating in a local caregiver support group to interact with others, share experiences, and gain social support. These meetings provide a platform for the caregiver to connect with others, offering emotional relief and a sense of belonging.

Whether virtual or in-person, connecting with others in the same boat can be helpful.

- ○ *Meaning-Making:* Draw meaning from the social connections and community you build in your caregiving role. Creating a blog or social media group to share their caregiving journey and connect with a wider community. This not only helps in documenting their experience but also allows them to reach out, engage with, and possibly inspire other caregivers, finding deeper meaning in their role through these connections.

Low Extraversion (Introversion)

Introverted caregivers may balk at the statistic that increasing numbers of care recipients are residing with their caregivers (AARP 2020). That said, introverted caregivers tend to prefer one-on-one interactions and may excel in providing deep, thoughtful care. They often find strength in quiet moments with the care recipient.

The potential drawbacks include feeling drained by extensive social coordination and a tendency to isolate, which can limit their support network and external caregiving resources.

- ○ *Interpersonal Communication:* Use written communication methods when face-to-face interactions are overwhelming. An introverted caregiver might prefer sending an email or text message to family members to update them about the care recipient's condition, instead of calling or organizing a family meeting. This allows them to communicate effectively without the drain of extended social interaction.

○ *Task Management:* Focus on one-on-one or behind-the-scenes tasks where you excel. Focus on tasks that require attention to detail and minimal social interaction, such as managing the care recipient's medication schedule or organizing medical records. These tasks allow the caregiver to work quietly and efficiently without the need for constant social engagement. Consider delegating more social tasks to others when possible.

○ *Emotional Well-being:* Create a quiet, personal space for relaxation away from caregiving duties. Creating a personal sanctuary in a specific room or corner of their house, where the caregiver can engage in solitary activities like reading, listening to music, or practicing meditation. This designated space provides a retreat for recharging away from caregiving duties. In a pinch, the bathroom can serve as a space of momentary reprieve; there you can take a few quiet, long breaths throughout the day.

○ *Meaning-Making:* Reflect on the depth and quality of care you provide in your one-on-one interactions. Keeping a personal journal where the introverted caregiver reflects on their caregiving experiences, focusing on the intimate and meaningful one-on-one moments spent with the care recipient. This practice helps in recognizing the value and depth of the care they provide, drawing meaning from these quieter, yet impactful interactions.

Agreeableness

High Agreeableness

Agreeableness (but not other traits) was found to protect the life satisfaction of individuals from stress associated with taking on caregiving duties (Hajek and König, 2018). Caregivers with high agreeableness are often also empathetic, cooperative, and nurturing. Such individuals were found to more easily focus on the rewarding aspects of caregiving (Koerner, Kenyon, & Shirai, 2009). They are adept at creating a supportive and caring environment and may excel in providing emotional support.

The challenge for highly agreeable caregivers is often in setting boundaries. They might neglect their own needs or struggle with assertively advocating for the care recipient's needs.

- *Interpersonal Communication:* Practice assertive communication to express your needs and opinions clearly. This facilitates your personal need being prioritized as well. For example, being clear in how you prioritize, such as saying, "I'm going to prioritize preparing your meals and managing your medications right now, as these are essential for your health. This means I may not be able to complete other tasks today, but it ensures I can give you the best support where it's needed most."

- *Task Management:* Learn to say no to tasks that are beyond your capacity. Agreeable people might find it hard to make decisions that could potentially disappoint or upset others, leading to indecision or defaulting to choices that may not be in their best interest. A simple 'no' is clear and doesn't need explanation, as hard as it may be to leave it at that.

- *Emotional Well-being:* Constantly adapting to others' preferences and needs can lead to a loss of personal identity or a sense of self, as agreeable individuals might suppress their true feelings or desires. Engage in activities that affirm your identity *outside of* caregiving, like a hobby or interest group. This helps maintain a sense of self and provides a much-needed break.

- *Meaning-Making:* Reflect on the compassion and empathy you bring to caregiving. Use your experiences to create a practical guide or resource for other caregivers, focus on efficient caregiving strategies, tips for navigating the healthcare system, and advocating for the care recipient.

Low Agreeableness:

Those on the lower end of agreeableness might bring a more pragmatic approach to caregiving. They may be good at making tough decisions and handling challenging situations without becoming overly emotional.

However, they might find it hard to express empathy and warmth. Their more direct approach could sometimes lead to conflicts with family members or healthcare professionals, or take on a more aggressive action/tone.

- ○ *Interpersonal Communication:* Work on active listening skills to improve empathy and understanding in conversations. Remember, listening doesn't mean agreeing; there's usually plenty of time to listen first and share your thoughts later; ask yourself if sharing them is necessary at that particular moment. This can improve relationships with the care recipient and other family members, making caregiving more harmonious.

- ○ *Task Management:* When collaborating with others in caregiving tasks, try to pause and show you (truly) value their input and perspectives. Alternatively, focus on tasks that require problem-solving or logistical planning, which aligns with the straightforward approach more common to those with low agreeableness. You might find satisfaction in efficiently organizing and managing care aspects.

- ○ *Emotional Well-being:* Practice stress-relief techniques that also enhance empathy, like guided empathy meditations. Alternatively, for those whose low agreeableness manifests from craving logic in their interactions with others, participating in a debate club or discussion group can provide a stimulating outlet away from caregiving duties, where intellectual discourse and argument are expected.

- ○ *Meaning-Making:* Acknowledge the strength and resilience you bring to caregiving, especially in tough decisions. Use your experiences to advocate for changes in caregiving policies in the community or within your support systems. This can be fulfilling and plays to strengths in directness and advocacy.

Neuroticism

High Neuroticism

One study found people high in neuroticism to be more likely to take on the task of caregiving (Rohr, Wagner, & Lang, 2013). Perhaps it's their attunement to the care recipient's needs and potential problems. Such individuals often demonstrate a high level of concern for the well-being of the person they are caring for. However, research finds that this attunement comes at a cost, such as increased negative emotional states and depression (Vinograd et al, 2020). Challenges include a tendency to experience heightened levels of stress, anxiety, and emotional exhaustion, which can lead to burnout. In addition to its direct impact on mental health, neuroticism has been found to have round-about effects (think of it like a domino effect) from the particular way people with high neuroticism think about their distress and burden (Pereira-Morales, Adan, & Forero, 2019). This can be helpful to consider, as it offers more opportunities for intervening in specific areas to positively impact the caregiver's well-being (a.k.a., more dominos to choose from).

- *Interpersonal Communication:* A caregiver with high neuroticism might react strongly to constructive feedback from healthcare professionals, perceiving it as criticism and responding defensively or with anxiety. This emotional reactivity can make effective communication difficult, potentially leading to misunderstandings or conflicts. Practice techniques like deep breathing or mindfulness before engaging in conversations, especially those that might be stressful. Consider role-playing with a therapist or trusted friend to prepare for potentially challenging interactions. This can help in responding more calmly and effectively.

- *Task Management:* Overwhelmed by the fear of making mistakes, a highly neurotic caregiver may double-check or triple-check medication dosages or constantly revisit care plans, even when they've been correctly handled. This excessive checking can be time-consuming, increase stress levels, and lead to inefficiency in caregiving duties. Create a daily checklist for caregiving tasks. Once a task is completed and checked off, practice trusting in the completion of the task. Use reminders or alarms as cues to move on to the next activity, preventing excessive rechecking.

- *Emotional Well-being:* Regularly practice relaxation techniques and consider professional support for managing stress. Schedule regular 'worry breaks' or journaling sessions where concerns are expressed and addressed, keeping the rest of the day more focused and less anxiety-driven. After a challenging day of caregiving, a caregiver with high neuroticism might lie awake worrying about the care recipient's future, their own performance, or potential health emergencies. Such persistent worries can lead to sleep disturbances, heightened stress, and an inability to relax and recharge. Incorporate relaxation techniques such as guided imagery, progressive muscle relaxation, or meditation into the daily routine, and at night when trying to fall asleep. Regular exercise can also be beneficial.

- *Meaning-Making:* There may be a tendency to dwell on negative aspects of caregiving, such as the challenges and sacrifices, rather than finding fulfillment in the role. This focus on the negative can prevent them from experiencing the rewarding aspects of caregiving and affect their overall satisfaction and sense of purpose. Keep a gratitude journal specifically related to caregiving, noting positive experiences, moments of connection, or successes, no matter how small. Joining a caregiver support group can provide a sense of community and offer a platform to share experiences and gain perspective. This can help shift focus from worries to the rewarding aspects of caregiving.

Low Neuroticism

Those with low levels of neuroticism usually handle the stresses of caregiving with more emotional stability and resilience. They tend to stay calm and composed in challenging situations.

On the flip side, they might be perceived as emotionally detached or less empathetic, which could impact the emotional aspect of caregiving and their relationships with the care recipient and family members.

- *Interpersonal Communication:* Your practical and straightforward communication style might sometimes be misinterpreted as insensitivity, especially in emotionally charged situations. Practice showing empathy and emotional support in conversations, even if they don't come naturally. Engage in active listening during conversations to ensure emotional support is provided where needed; to do this, pay full attention when others are speaking, face them when speaking/listening, ask open-ended questions, and reflect back what you've heard to demonstrate understanding. This can enhance empathy and understanding in caregiver-care recipient interactions.

- *Task Management:* The belief in your ability to cope with any situation might lead to underestimating your personal limits, risking burnout. On the flip side, you may excel at taking on roles that require a calm and steady approach, which might be challenging for others, such as handling emergencies or difficult healthcare negotiations.

- *Emotional Well-being:* Your ability to remain calm and composed might make it challenging to relate to or understand the stress and anxiety experienced by others, including family members or the care recipient. Try gradually sharing personal thoughts and feelings. Self-disclosure should be reciprocal and grow with the depth of the relationship.

- ○ *Meaning-Making:* Appreciate the stability and calmness your approach brings to the caregiving environment. Caregivers with low neuroticism might be seen as emotionally detached or less empathetic, especially by those who expect a more overt emotional response to caregiving challenges. There is usually space for both practicality and the emotions that color our daily experiences.

For caregivers with low neuroticism, balancing their natural tendency towards emotional stability with an understanding of the emotional aspects of caregiving is crucial. This involves actively working on empathy, acknowledging their emotional needs, and being open to seeking and accepting support.

By understanding these traits and their extremes, caregivers can better recognize their natural inclinations, strengths, and areas where they might need to adapt or seek support. This awareness can lead to more effective and balanced caregiving.

The Meaning of Meaning-making

One of the areas you just read about, *meaning-making*, has been researched for its protective effect on emotional wellbeing and psychological health; research efforts have even been specific to caregivers. Meaning-making, being that it is more abstract, often takes the backseat to the more concrete and pressing concerns of caregiving (e.g., task management); meanwhile, it can be an untapped resource for caregivers.

An effective therapy technique–Meaning-Centered Psychotherapy for Caregivers (MCPC)–was developed to assist caregivers in connecting to meaning and purpose despite the demands of caregiving (Applebaum et al, 2022). It provides interventions informed by the meaning derived from one's legacies (past, present, and future), attitudes, creative living (commitment to valued activities), and present-moment experiences (via the senses, love, beauty and humor). Based on conversation with one of its developers, the benefits of MCPC have not been examined for links to caregiver personality traits. However, the approach is considered transdiagnostic, which means it addresses symptoms experienced across various diagnoses. For this reason, it is included in this section on personality, instead of a previous chapter on a specific disorder. We incorporate a few of the interventions in this book, but more details about the approach can be found in the therapy manual (Applebaum & Breitbart, 2024).

Becoming You

Our personalities evolve over time, with much influence from our experiences. One intervention from MCPC that taps into the creation of this sense of self is the Life Review exercise. This exercise is best done with the help of a therapist trained in this approach, but the general ideas will be shared here so you can see its potential as a resource. Caregivers begin by reflecting on key stages or moments in their life, such as childhood, adolescence, adulthood, and their caregiving journey. For example, a caregiver might identify a defining moment from their youth, like learning responsibility early by helping in the family business, which now informs their sense of duty in caregiving.

Next, they explore sources of strength by recalling challenges they've overcome and the lessons learned. A caregiver might reflect on a time when they managed a difficult family crisis, realizing that their problem-solving skills and emotional resilience are invaluable assets in their current role. The exercise then shifts to connecting these past experiences to caregiving, helping caregivers recognize how their history shapes their approach to caregiving. For instance, someone may realize that their value of compassion, cultivated through years of volunteer work, aligns deeply with the care they now provide.

Finally, caregivers reflect on the legacy they hope to create, identifying ways caregiving contributes to their loved one's life and their own sense of purpose. A response might include, "I hope my care shows my loved one how deeply they are valued, and that I'll be remembered for showing patience and kindness." Through this process, caregivers can uncover meaning, appreciate their growth, and strengthen their identity as an individual and as a caregiver.

Resources for Caregiver Personalities

1. **Support Groups**: In-person and online support communities have their own unique dynamics, thus catering

to caregivers with different temperaments. Finding a group that aligns with your personality style can provide invaluable emotional support and insights. It can be helpful to try out a couple, until you find one that fits.

2. **Personality Assessments**: Tools like the Big Five personality traits assessment can help caregivers gain self-awareness and adapt their caregiving approach accordingly. Sometimes you have a hunch as to where your preferences lie, but you may just be surprised by the results! Consult with a psychologist to get a more accurate assessment.

3. **Counseling and Therapy**: Professional counseling or therapy can be especially beneficial for caregivers struggling with the emotional aspects of caregiving. A trained therapist can help individuals manage their personality-related challenges.

4. **Books and Literature**: There are numerous books tailored to different personality types, offering guidance and strategies based on temperament. They don't typically relate directly to caregiving, but the tips within can often be translated to caregiving and well-being.

By recognizing the influence of temperament and personality on the caregiving journey, individuals can adapt their approaches, manage their outlook, and create a caregiving experience that aligns with their unique traits. The key is to embrace self-awareness, seek support, and prioritize self-care, ultimately fostering a healthier and more fulfilling caregiving experience.

Perfectionism in Caregiving

"Have no fear of perfection—you'll never reach it."

- Salvador Dali

Another personality trait that doesn't quite fit within the Big Five review we just did is perfectionism. Here, the pursuit of perfection meets the inherently imperfect nature of caregiving. Caregivers with perfectionistic tendencies may strive to provide the best possible care, often going above and beyond. However, this pursuit can also lead to excessive self-criticism, fear of making mistakes, and burnout. Through this chapter, we explore how perfectionism manifests in caregiving and strategies for managing these challenges while harnessing the positive aspects of striving for excellence.

Understanding Perfectionism in Caregiving

Perfectionism in caregiving can manifest in various ways, including:

1. **Excessive Concern Over Mistakes**: Fear of making errors in caregiving tasks, leading to constant checking and rechecking.

2. **High Personal Standards**: Setting unrealistically high standards for oneself as a caregiver, often leading to feelings of inadequacy.

3. **Overcommitment**: Taking on too many responsibilities or tasks in an attempt to provide perfect care.

4. **Critical Self-Evaluation**: Harsh self-criticism over perceived caregiving failures or shortcomings.

5. **Fear of Judgment**: Worrying excessively about what others think of their caregiving skills.

A Caregiving Story: Perfection & Parkinson's

Sophia's role as a caregiver for her mother, grappling with the challenges of Parkinson's disease, was colored by her lifelong struggle with perfectionism.

Sophia's perfectionism wasn't just a personality quirk; it was a deeply ingrained part of her identity, rooted in her childhood. Growing up as the eldest daughter in a family where academic and extracurricular excellence were not just encouraged but expected, Sophia learned early on that her achievements were a source of pride for her parents. Her self-worth became tightly intertwined with her ability to perform tasks flawlessly, whether in school or at home.

When her mother's health began to decline, Sophia stepped into the role of caregiver with a sense of duty and an unconscious desire to uphold her image of perfection. She meticulously managed every aspect of her mother's care, from medication schedules to physical therapy sessions, often going beyond what was required to ensure everything was done perfectly.

The tipping point came unexpectedly. It wasn't a missed medication or a doctor's appointment but something more personal. In her relentless focus on her mother's health, Sophia forgot her parents' wedding anniversary - an event she had always orchestrated with love and care. This oversight hit her hard. It was a stark reminder that in her pursuit of caregiving perfection, she was losing sight of the little personal touches that brought joy to her and her family.

This realization forced Sophia to confront the unsustainable nature of her approach to caregiving and the perfectionism that drove it.

Sophia's path to change began with counseling. In her sessions, she delved into the roots of her perfectionism, understanding how her childhood perspective had set unrealistic standards that she constantly strived to meet. The counselor helped her see that her worth wasn't tied to her ability to be a perfect caregiver. They used techniques from acceptance and commitment therapy, such as reflecting on the importance of being seen as perfect versus the value of a strong relationship.

Sophia started to implement practical changes in her daily routine. She set more achievable goals for each day and began to (reluctantly at first) forgive herself for the occasional lapse. She also started a journal, not just to log caregiving activities but to express her feelings and reflections. This journal became a safe space for her to process her thoughts and recognize her achievements.

Joining a local support group for caregivers of Parkinson's patients opened Sophia's eyes to the diverse ways people cope with caregiving challenges. She found comfort in sharing her experiences and learning from others. It was in these meetings that Sophia learned the value of emotional support over logistical perfection.

Sophia also learned to delegate. She hired a part-time caregiver to assist with her mother's care. Initially, relinquishing control was difficult, but seeing her mother engage positively with another caregiver was reassuring and helped alleviate some of Sophia's self-imposed pressure. (She had been telling herself that she didn't think her mother would be comfortable with formal caregivers in the home, but the reality was quite the opposite.)

Over time, Sophia began to embrace the beauty in imperfection. She found joy in moments that were not planned, like impromptu afternoon teas with her mother, filled with laughter and reminiscing. She learned to value the quality of these moments over the quest for perfection in their execution. She found herself thinking, "So what if we don't have milk for one day, we can still enjoy this experience."

Sophia's story highlights the importance of understanding the roots of our actions and beliefs and shows that in caregiving, as in life, perfection is not the goal — connection, love, and presence are.

Consequences of Perfectionism in Caregiving

Perfectionism in caregiving can have significant consequences, impacting both the caregiver and the care recipient. While striving for high standards is not inherently negative, perfectionism often involves unrealistic expectations and an inability to accept mistakes, which can lead to physical, emotional, and relational challenges.

1. **Emotional Exhaustion and Burnout**: Perfectionist caregivers often push themselves to meet unattainable standards, refusing to delegate tasks or take breaks. This leads to chronic stress and emotional fatigue. Caregivers may feel overwhelmed, resentful, or even detached from the care recipient due to the constant pressure they place on themselves.

2. **Increased Anxiety and Self-Doubt**: The fear of making mistakes or not being "good enough" can cause persistent worry and undermine confidence. Caregivers may ruminate on minor errors or perceived shortcomings. Anxiety can impair decision-making, making caregiving tasks more stressful and less effective.

3. **Strained Relationships**: Perfectionism can lead caregivers to criticize themselves or others for not meeting unrealistic expectations. This can create tension with family members, the care recipient, or other support systems. Caregivers may become

isolated, reluctant to ask for help, or overly controlling, which can harm trust and cooperation.

4. **Neglect of Self-Care**: Caregivers focused on achieving perfection often prioritize caregiving tasks over their own well-being, skipping meals, sleep, or social activities to "do it all." Neglecting self-care can lead to physical health problems, weakened immunity, and increased risk of depression.

5. **Reduced Flexibility and Problem-Solving Ability**: A perfectionist mindset can make caregivers overly rigid, focusing on doing things "the right way" rather than adapting to changes or finding practical solutions. This rigidity can create unnecessary stress and prevent caregivers from embracing simpler, more effective approaches.

6. **Loss of Joy in Caregiving**: The constant pressure to be flawless can overshadow the meaningful and rewarding aspects of caregiving. Caregiving may begin to feel like an unmanageable burden rather than a fulfilling role, leading to disengagement or emotional detachment.'

7. **Negative Impact on the Care Recipient**: A caregiver's perfectionism can unintentionally create stress for the care recipient, who may feel they are a source of constant pressure or inadequacy. This can lead to a strained caregiver-care recipient relationship

and reduce the recipient's sense of independence and autonomy.

8. **Difficulty Delegating or Accepting Help**: Perfectionists may believe no one else can provide care to their high standards, avoiding delegation or rejecting offers of assistance. This isolates the caregiver, increases their workload, and prevents others from contributing to the caregiving process.

While perfectionism may stem from a desire to provide excellent care, it often leads to emotional and physical harm for caregivers and can negatively impact the care recipient. Addressing perfectionist tendencies by setting realistic goals, accepting help, and practicing self-compassion is essential for fostering a healthier caregiving experience.

Caregiving Issues and Solutions for Perfectionists

1. **Setting Realistic Expectations**: Acknowledge that perfection in caregiving is unattainable. Setting achievable goals involves a shift in mindset and practical strategies:

    o   <u>Setting Boundaries</u>: Clearly define limits to caregiving responsibilities to prevent overcommitment, curb expectations, and ensure personal well-being. E.g., you'll manage meals and medications, but someone else takes care of finances.

    o   <u>Redefine Success</u>: Begin by redefining what success means in the context of your situation. Understand that perfection is unattainable and that 'good enough' can often be the most realistic and healthy goal. Defining exactly where 'good enough' lies means there is an actual point where you can somewhat relax.

- o Learn from Feedback, Not Failure: View mistakes or shortcomings as opportunities for learning and improvement ("growth mindset"), not as failures. This perspective encourages adaptation and reduces the pressure for perfection. Those with a growth mindset are more likely to persist when faced with difficult problems compared to those with a fixed mindset (Zhao et al., 2021).

- o Break Down Goals: Set small, manageable goals instead of broad, ambitious ones. Breaking down tasks into smaller, achievable steps makes them less overwhelming and more attainable.

- o Realistic Expectations: Assess your resources, time, and capabilities realistically. Set goals that are attainable with what you have, not idealistic targets that require unrealistic efforts.

- o Prioritize Tasks: Identify what's truly important and focus on these areas. Not all tasks require the same level of attention and perfection. Learn to prioritize based on impact and necessity.

- o Celebrate Small Wins: Acknowledge and celebrate even the small achievements. This reinforces the satisfaction of meeting goals and helps shift the focus from perfection to progress.

o Time Management: Allocate a realistic amount of time for tasks, including a buffer for unforeseen issues. This helps in setting achievable deadlines and reduces the urge to rush to perfection.

o Practice Self-Compassion: Be kind to yourself. Recognize that striving for perfection is often more self-critical than productive. Self-compassion involves understanding that it's okay not to be perfect.

o Mindfulness and Reflection: Engage in mindfulness practices to stay present and reduce worries about perfection. Reflect on your accomplishments and efforts at the end of the day or week.

o Seek Feedback: Get input from others. Sometimes, an external perspective can help you see that your efforts are sufficient and valued, even if they don't meet your internal standards of perfection.

o Adjust Goals as Needed: Be flexible and willing to adjust your goals as circumstances change. Flexibility is key to setting realistic goals and accepting 'good enough.'

o Limit Comparison: Avoid comparing your achievements or progress to others. Focus on your journey and growth.

- Focus on the Process, Not Just the Outcome: Enjoy and learn from the process of working towards your goals. This can shift the focus from achieving a perfect outcome to valuing the experience and learning it brings.

  By implementing these strategies, you can cultivate a healthier approach to goal setting and learn to embrace 'good enough', reducing the stress and unrealistic expectations often associated with perfectionism.

2. **Dealing with Fear of Mistakes**: Understand that mistakes are part of the learning process. Develop a system for double-checking important tasks without obsessing over them. Creating a system to double-check important tasks without falling into the trap of obsessing over them involves striking a balance between thoroughness and efficiency. Here's a structured approach to achieve this:

   - Clearly Define Caregiving Tasks: Clearly outline what each caregiving task involves and what successful completion looks like. For example, if the task is medication management, define the exact dosage and times. This clarity reduces uncertainty and helps you know exactly what to check.

   - Set Specific Times for Review: Allocate specific times to review and double-check caregiving tasks. For instance, you might check that medications have been administered correctly immediately after doing so, then do a daily end-of-day review of all tasks completed.

o   Limit the Number of Reviews: Decide beforehand how many times you will review each caregiving task. Limiting this to one or two reviews can prevent the cycle of obsessive over-checking. Trust in the initial completion of the task.

o   Plan for Mistakes: Accept that mistakes can occur in caregiving and have a plan for addressing them if they happen. For example, know the steps to take if a medication dose is missed or a doctor's appointment is forgotten.

o   Involve a Second Person for Critical Caregiving Tasks: For important tasks, such as administering medication, involve another family member or a professional caregiver for double-checking. This can provide peace of mind and reduce the fear of making critical mistakes.

o   Reflect on Past Outcomes of Caregiving Tasks: Regularly assess how effective your double-checking system is. Reflect on past caregiving tasks to see if your methods are working or if you need to make any adjustments.

o   Practice Letting Go After Checking: Once you've completed your checks, consciously practice letting go of the worry. Reassure yourself that you have done what is needed and that excessive checking is not helpful. Say something to yourself like, "Even the best work has room for improvement. What I've done is surely adequate for what's needed."

○ <u>Seek Feedback on Your Caregiving System</u>: Feedback from the care recipient through tools like the Values and Preferences scale (doctorolson.com/care) can give confidence that you're addressing the important things (according to the care recipient), so you can relax or use your energy more wisely. Or periodically get feedback from someone you trust, like a family member, friend, or healthcare professional. They can provide an outside perspective on whether your checking system is appropriate or if it seems excessive. This can be another benefit of joining a caregiver support group. It is often helpful to see how often others make a "mistake" to get a benchmark for what is reasonable to expect out of yourself.

○ <u>Redefine Perfect</u>: If you lean towards perfectionism, it's likely that this has been part of your approach for a long time. It can be hard to just shake off being a perfectionist. Instead of trying to "stop" being perfect at a task, try redefining what perfect means. For example, instead of telling yourself that you must administer every dose within 5 minutes of schedule and never miss a dose, try redefining perfect as 1) being on the lookout for mistakes, or 2) quickly recovering after a mistake, or perhaps 3) learning to get more efficient each time you do something. If you define perfect as catching mistakes, then when you catch your mistake, you can celebrate the success of catching it (and managing what to do for a missed dose), rather than feeling like you failed because you made a mistake in the first place.

3. **Managing Critical Self-Evaluation**: Practice self-compassion and recognize the hard work and dedication involved in caregiving. (See the section on Inner Critic on page 35.) One strategy that can bolster self-compassion comes from Meaning-Centered Psychotherapy and focuses on connecting your beliefs to your values. First, explore your values (beyond striving for perfection!), such as through journaling, using a values-sort app, or having a chat with a loved one or therapist. Once you've clarified your values, you can more easily identify how your beliefs align (or don't align) with your personal values and caregiving goals (e.g., "I value patience and connection. How can I let go of perfectionism to honor those values?").

4. **Coping with Fear of Judgment**: Build confidence in caregiving abilities and remind oneself that external opinions are not a reflection of one's worth or competence. Let's review some strategies of how to go about doing this:

    o   <u>Cultivate Self-Awareness</u>: Take time to reflect on your values, beliefs, and priorities as a caregiver.

Understanding what matters most to you in your caregiving role will help you stay focused on your goals and be less influenced by others' opinions about how caregiving should be done. Consider partaking in the values sort app mentioned above.

- Strengthen Self-Confidence in Your Caregiving Abilities: Build confidence in your caregiving skills and judgments. Acknowledge and celebrate the successes you've had in caring for your loved one. Learn from any mistakes, understanding that they are part of the caregiving journey. This confidence comes from recognizing your competence and trusting in your ability to make good decisions for your care recipient.

- Differentiate Opinion from Fact in Advice: When receiving advice or comments about your caregiving, remember that opinions are not facts. They are subjective and based on the individual perspectives of those giving them. Distinguish between what is opinion and what is factual information.

- Seek Constructive Feedback, Not Approval: Aim to get constructive feedback that can help you improve your caregiving, rather than seeking approval or validation from others. Constructive feedback can provide valuable insights and help you grow as a caregiver.

- ○ <u>Surround Yourself with Supportive People</u>: Choose to spend time with people who support and uplift your caregiving efforts. Avoid those who are consistently negative or critical, as they can undermine your confidence and well-being.

- ○ <u>Reflect on the Source of Opinions About Your Caregiving</u>: Consider who is giving opinions about your caregiving and why. Often, people project their own insecurities or biases. Understanding this can diminish the impact of their opinions on your caregiving choices.

- ○ <u>Acknowledge External Influences on Caregiving Perceptions</u>: Recognize how societal and cultural norms might influence your perception of others' opinions regarding caregiving. Challenge any societal expectations that don't align with your personal caregiving values and situation.

- ○ <u>Focus on What You Can Control in Caregiving</u>: Understand that you can't control what others think about your caregiving, but you can control your reaction and how you let it affect you. Direct your energy toward aspects of caregiving that you can influence and improve.

Conclusion

Caregiving with perfectionistic tendencies is a path of balancing the drive for excellence with the acceptance of caregiving's unpredictable and imperfect nature. It involves understanding the limitations of what can be controlled, practicing self-compassion, and learning to value progress over perfection. By adopting strategies to manage perfectionism, caregivers can find a more sustainable and fulfilling approach to caregiving, one that honors both their commitment to providing high-quality care and their own well-being.

A Note on Overlapping Conditions

Being diagnosed with two or more psychiatric disorders is actually nearly as common as having solely one diagnosis. Managing overlapping health conditions such as ADHD and depression while undertaking caregiving responsibilities is tricky. Caregivers juggle their personal health needs while ensuring they provide effective care to their loved ones. The key lies in acknowledging the interplay between personal health and caregiving duties. For instance, the structured routines beneficial for ADHD management can also lend stability in managing depression and caregiving tasks. Mental health underpins handling caregiving responsibilities effectively; it is supported by regular therapy, medication management, and stress-reduction activities.

Time management strategies are crucial, and facilitated by tools such as planners and apps. Communication with the care recipient, when feasible, about one's limitations and needs can help set realistic expectations and foster mutual understanding. Moreover, practicing self-compassion is vital. Caregivers facing dual-diagnoses should recognize the enormity of their task and give themselves grace on challenging days. Seeking support, whether from friends, family, or professionals, and being open to delegating tasks, can also alleviate the burden.

In sum, caregivers who consider their personality and mental health conditions while providing care set themselves up for a smoother caregiving experience. This venture is one of continuous learning, adaptation, and self-discovery.

Versatile Strategies

Some strategies are one-trick ponies, but others can help across a variety of contexts or a variety of mental health conditions. Below are a few of the latter to help manage emotions and energy when caregiving. Not all may be possible, depending on your situation, but see if one or more can be applied to your practice of caring for yourself and others.

Gauging Care Alignment

This may sound familiar, as the approach was previously mentioned in the section on anxiety. It is advantageous for most if not all caregiving relationships to have a tool for gauging care alignment. The Values and Preferences Scale (Whitlatch, Feinberg, & Tucke, 2005) was designed to highlight areas that the care recipient values more or less than the caregiver. With this information, you can then adjust your approach on tasks to optimize alignment, such as opting for more time on reaching out to family members and less on co-managing finances.

You can find the interactive questionnaire at doctorolson.com/care and be provided with suggested adjustments and other tips after submitting your responses. The feedback provided highlights areas that may benefit from some adjustment in day-to-day practices and ways to discuss these topics constructively.

Create a Caregiving Container

No, this isn't a tip jar. It's a practice in setting a time and space for discussing caregiving plans and duties. This will look different for each person, but the big idea is to guard time and space so that caregiving tasks don't crop up anywhere and at any time. We are creatures of habit, which means we like predictability. It allows us to prepare accordingly. If you can, set a time and/or a place where caregiving tasks happen. Your mind and body, such priceless personal resources (like your attention, focus, memory, or problem-solving capacity), will thank you because they can now rest within that space. This also relieves stress during the rest of your day, as you know that what needs to get done will get done, when it is time, not now while you need to focus on something else.

One example of this practice is only talking about doctor appointments in the evening when seated on a certain couch. The rest of the day, and in the rest of the house, your body knows it can relax, or at least not be taxed by the demands of coordinating doctor appointments (or whatever you delegate to that time and space).

Check out this example of a real-life Caregiving Container:

> Jenny, a caregiver for her aging mother, decided to use her sunroom every Tuesday evening as her caregiving container. During this time, she reviews her mother's medical needs, schedules appointments, and plans the week's caregiving tasks. Once she leaves the sunroom,

she allows herself to shift focus away from caregiving responsibilities, knowing that this space and time are dedicated to managing these demands. Occasionally, she weaves in specific additional times, such as 1-hour after lunch for returning phone calls or researching latest treatments. This is also done in the sunroom. This practice helps Jenny maintain a sense of control and balance in her life.

A few steps can help in implementing the Caregiving Container:

1. **Scheduling Discussions**: Set a recurring time, such as every evening or a specific day of the week, dedicated exclusively to caregiving discussions and planning.

2. **Designating Spaces**: Choose a particular area in your home, such as a home office or a specific corner in the living room, where caregiving tasks are addressed.

3. **Limiting Caregiving Talk**: Enforce the rule that outside of these times and spaces, caregiving topics are not to be discussed. This helps in mentally compartmentalizing caregiving responsibilities.

4. **Mindful Transitions**: Engage in a brief mindfulness practice or relaxation technique before entering and after leaving your caregiving container space, to help transition in and out of the caregiving role.

5. **Recording Thoughts and Tasks**: If caregiving thoughts come to mind outside of the designated times,

jot them down in a notebook or digital app to be addressed during the next scheduled caregiving time.

The caregiving container is a practical approach to creating boundaries that protect your mental and emotional well-being. It enables you to manage caregiving responsibilities more effectively while preserving space for personal relaxation and rejuvenation. Again, it will look different for everyone. Sometimes it won't be practical to limit phone calls to one hour a week. That's okay, try shaping the container as best you can. That might mean every other day or a few hours out of the day for a certain task. Give it a try.

Celebrating Small Successes

Celebrating small successes is a vital part of maintaining a positive outlook and motivation in caregiving. Celebrating small successes as a caregiver can involve recognizing and appreciating specific achievements, no matter how modest they may seem. Here are concrete examples of these successes and how they can be celebrated:

1. **Successful Doctor's Visit:**

    - Example: The caregiver successfully managed a catastrophe-free doctor's visit for the care recipient, including timely medication administration and transportation.

    - Celebration: As simple as a high five with the care recipient or a friend, marking the occasion with a favorite snack on the way home, or even simply pausing to tell yourself "nice job!"

2. **Completing All Medications on Time:**

   - <u>Example</u>: For a week straight, the caregiver ensured all medications were given on time without any misses. (If your inner critic is now saying, "But that's what I'm supposed to do, why would I celebrate it?" Then see the section on Inner Critic below on page 35.)

   - <u>Celebration</u>: Taking a relaxing bath at the end of the week or enjoying a favorite movie.

3. **Improvement in the Care Recipient's Mood or Health:**

   - <u>Example</u>: The care recipient shows signs of improved mood or health, perhaps smiling more or engaging in a conversation.

   - <u>Celebration</u>: Sharing a special dessert or a small party with family to acknowledge this improvement.

4. **Handling a Difficult Situation Well:**

   - <u>Example</u>: The caregiver managed a challenging behavior or medical emergency calmly and effectively.

- Celebration: Journaling about the experience to reflect on the success and sharing the story with a supportive friend or family member.

5. **Teaching the Care Recipient a New Skill**:

   - Example: The caregiver successfully teaches the care recipient how to use a new device, like a smartphone or a remote control.

   - Celebration: Taking a moment to enjoy a shared hobby or activity as a reward for both.

6. **Maintaining a Clean and Organized Living Space**:

   - Example: Keeping the care recipient's living space clean and organized for a period of time, e.g., a month.

   - Celebration: Buying a small plant or decorative item or picking a few flowers to further enhance the living space.

7. **Effective Communication with Healthcare Professionals**:

   - Example: The caregiver effectively communicates the care recipient's needs and concerns during a healthcare appointment, leading to a positive outcome.

   - Celebration: Enjoying a favorite podcast or music album as a personal reward.

8. **Implementing a New Care Strategy Successfully:**

   - ○ <u>Example</u>: Introducing a new dietary plan or exercise routine that benefits the care recipient.

   - ○ <u>Celebration</u>: Sharing the success with an online caregiver community or support group.

9. **Taking Time for Self-Care:**

   - ○ <u>Example</u>: The caregiver manages to take regular short breaks throughout the week for self-care.

   - ○ <u>Celebration</u>: Treating themselves to a tea or smoothie at a favorite café or a leisurely walk in a park.

10. **Positive Feedback from the Care Recipient:**

   - ○ <u>Example</u>: Receiving a word of thanks or appreciation from the care recipient or their family.

   - ○ <u>Celebration</u>: Writing down these words in a gratitude journal to look back on during tougher days.

By acknowledging and celebrating these small but significant achievements, caregivers can cultivate a sense of accomplishment and maintain motivation. These celebrations, whether they are moments of self-care or shared joy with the care recipient, reinforce the positive impact of such hard work and dedication.

Open Dialogues

Open communication is a powerful tool that can transform the caregiving experience, providing caregivers with emotional relief, practical clarity, and personal growth opportunities. By fostering honest dialogue, caregivers can reduce stress, better understand care recipients' needs, and strengthen their relationship. Open communication also encourages mutual feedback, allowing caregivers to receive validation for their efforts and learn new approaches to caregiving. It helps prioritize tasks, manage time more effectively, and establish healthy boundaries, preventing burnout. Ultimately, embracing open communication creates a more balanced, supportive caregiving dynamic, benefiting both the caregiver and the care recipient. Below are a few thoughtful and respectful ways to initiate this conversation. Consider using one of the following prompts after completing the previously mentioned Values and Preferences scale, which can be found at doctorolson.com/care:

1. **Open-Ended Inquiry**: "I'd love to hear how you feel about the care I'm providing. What are some things that you enjoy and is there anything you think we could change?"

2. **Specific Feedback Request**: "Can you tell me how you feel about our morning/evening routine? I want to make sure our routine is as comfortable yet effective as possible."

3. **Regular Check-Ins**: "Let's do our weekly check-in. How are you feeling about everything? Are there areas where you feel we could make some adjustments?"

4. **Feedback on Changes**: "I noticed you seemed [describe observation here] after we changed [specific aspect]. How has that been working out for you? Should we keep it this way or try something else?"

5. **Encouragement for Open Dialogue**: "Please feel free to share your thoughts about how things are going. Your comfort and happiness are very important to me. What's working well for you, and what isn't?"

These approaches foster an open dialogue, making the care recipient feel valued and respected, and provide critical feedback to help tailor care to their specific needs and preferences.

Clockwork Self-care

Below are some ways of weaving in self-care on a regular basis:

1. <u>Establish a Routine</u>: Develop a daily or weekly routine that includes dedicated time slots (even 5 or 10 minutes) for self-care activities. Having a structured schedule can help ensure that self-care is a regular part of the caregiver's life.

2. <u>Integrate Self-Care into the Caregiving Routine</u>: Look for ways to incorporate self-care into the existing caregiving

routine. For example, if the caregiver enjoys exercise, they could go for walks with their care recipient if possible or watch a documentary that aligns with their own interests.

3. <u>Practice Micro Self-Care</u>: Similarly, engage in "micro" self-care activities that take little time but are beneficial, such as meditation, deep breathing exercises, or slowly sipping a cup of tea. Another example is a mini stretch session, such as repeating 30 seconds of stretching between each task during the hour.

4. <u>Use Technology to Save Time</u>: Employ technology to streamline caregiving tasks. For example, setting up automatic medication reminders, online grocery delivery, or telehealth appointments (instead of in-person) can reduce the time spent on these tasks. (See the Technology section on page 184.)

5. <u>Prioritize and Limit Activities</u>: Evaluate and prioritize caregiving tasks. Focus on essential tasks and consider which ones can be simplified or eliminated.

6. <u>Seek Financial Assistance for Caregiving</u>: If financial constraints are a barrier to accessing respite care, explore options for financial assistance. Some organizations offer grants or subsidies for caregivers, and certain insurance plans may cover respite care services.

Prioritizing Tasks: An Example

You'll find more on prioritizing tasks in the section on ADHD (page 3). Here, let's consider an example of prioritizing caregiving tasks for an elderly parent with diabetes and limited mobility. The caregiver needs to manage a variety of tasks, ranging from medical care to personal and household duties.

1. Morning Medication and Blood Sugar Check (Urgent and Important):

   - First, assist the parent with their morning medication, crucial for managing diabetes.

2. Perform a blood sugar check to ensure levels are within a safe range.

3. Breakfast Preparation (Important):

   - Prepare a healthy breakfast that aligns with dietary needs for diabetes.

   - Assist them with eating if necessary.

4. Personal Hygiene (Important):

   - Help the parent with morning personal hygiene routines such as bathing, brushing teeth, and getting dressed. This is important for their comfort and dignity.

5. Physical Therapy Exercises (Important):

- o   Assist the parent with prescribed physical therapy exercises to maintain mobility and prevent muscle atrophy.

6. Medical Appointment (Urgent and Important on Specific Days):

- o   If scheduled, transport and accompany the parent to any medical appointments. These are critical for monitoring their health condition.

7. Household Chores (Less Urgent):

- o   Perform household tasks such as laundry, cleaning, or tidying up. While these are important, they are less urgent and can be adjusted based on other priorities.

8. Lunch Preparation (Important):

- o   Prepare a nutritious lunch, keeping in mind the dietary restrictions and preferences.

9. Social Interaction and Leisure (Important for Quality of Life):

- o   Dedicate time for social interaction, such as having a conversation, playing a game, or engaging in a shared hobby. This is crucial for emotional well-being but can be flexible throughout the day.

10. Afternoon Medication and Blood Sugar Check (Urgent and Important):

- o Administer any afternoon medication and perform another blood sugar check.

11. Evening Care (Important):

   - o Assist with dinner preparation and ensure the parent eats a balanced meal.

   - o Help with the nighttime personal care routine, including getting ready for bed.

12. Prepare for the Next Day (Less Urgent):

   - o Plan and organize for the next day's tasks, such as setting out clothes or prepping meal ingredients.

13. Self-Care (Important):

   - o Allocate time for personal self-care activities to prevent caregiver burnout.

In this example, the caregiver prioritizes tasks based on urgency and importance, ensuring that critical health-related tasks are addressed first while also balancing personal care, household duties, and their own well-being. This approach ensures that the parent's essential needs are met while maintaining a manageable routine for the caregiver.

Task Management Template

Below is a template for you to use to enhance task management. Each row represents a separate task/subtask or activity that needs to be completed. Group similar tasks together to provide structure and make it easier to manage similar activities at once. If you're having trouble managing tasks, I offer a brief series of sessions geared toward learning tools for task management for caregivers–just reach out to me at doctorolson.com. One-on-one consultation can help personalize these strategies to your needs.

Task Chart

Task Description	Priority	Who	Time	Due	Status	Notes
New medical equipment						
Ask about nebulizer	Medium	Nurse	5 min.	Friday		
See if shower chair fits	High	Me	10 min.	Monday	X	
Schedule physical therapist	High	Me	15 min.	Thursday	IP	Left voicemail

Details for each column are below:

- **Task Description**: Clearly describe the task. Use clear but concise language.

- **Priority Level**:
  - Write High, Medium, Low to indicate how urgent or important a task is.
  - Color-coding can also be beneficial here for quick visual reference.

- **Who/Assigned To**: If the caregiving responsibilities are shared, indicate who is responsible for each task. This helps in managing accountability and dividing the workload effectively. Alternatively, you can also write if there are specific people needed for the task, such as the example filled in on the chart above with the nurse, meaning the nurse's input is needed.

- **Due Date/Time**: Specify when the task needs to be completed. Offering a visual timeline or calendar view next to the due date can help in better time management.

- **Time Estimate**: Include an estimate of how long the task is expected to take. This aids in planning out the day more effectively, considering ADHD-related time management challenges. It can also help with motivation, since seeing a task is likely to take 5 minutes (e.g., a phone call) can make it feel easy to squeeze in here or there.

- **Status**: Use simple categories like "Not Started" (or just write "NS"), "In Progress" ("IP"), "Completed" ("X"), or "Deferred" ("Wait") to track the progress of each task. Visual cues such as checkboxes or icons can be effective here. If it seems fun, use a stamp to mark it done or a sticker (yes, it's childish, but a touch of fun).

- **Notes**: Provide space for any additional details, reminders, or specific instructions related to the task. This is also a good place to jot down any changes or updates to the task as they occur. For more extensive notes, you can write "see notebook" and expand on notes or plans in a separate notebook.

Additional Features for ADHD:

- Color Coding: Assign colors to different categories of tasks (e.g., personal care, medical appointments, household chores) for quick identification.

- Checklists: For complex tasks, break them down into smaller, actionable steps in a checklist format. This can help in overcoming procrastination by making tasks appear more manageable.

- Flexible Layout: Consider leaving some blank spaces or "flex slots" for tasks that may arise spontaneously throughout the day. This caters to the flexible nature of caregiving and the unpredictable challenges that may emerge.

- Visual Timers and Alerts: Incorporating the use of timers for time-sensitive tasks or for managing breaks can help in maintaining focus and managing time effectively.

- Review Section: At the end of the planner or day, include a brief section for reflection. This can be used to jot down what went well, what could be improved, and any insights gained throughout the day.

Know Your Limits

While it's important to challenge yourself, it's equally important to balance ambition with a realistic understanding of what can be achieved given your current situation. Determining the limits of what you can accomplish involves self-awareness and an understanding of your capabilities, resources, and circumstances. Here's how someone can assess and understand their limits:

- **Self-Reflection**: Engage in regular self-reflection to evaluate your strengths, weaknesses, energy levels, and skills. Be honest about what you can realistically manage.

- **Feedback from Past Experiences**: Look back at past experiences to identify when you've felt overextended or particularly successful. Learn from these instances to gauge your capacity for different tasks.

- **Physical and Emotional Signals**: Pay attention to physical and emotional signs of stress or burnout. Persistent fatigue, anxiety, or a decline in health can signal that you're pushing beyond your limits.

- **Set Small, Achievable Goals**: Start with small goals and gradually increase the complexity or scale. This helps you understand your capacity for achievement without becoming overwhelmed.

- **Ask for Input**: Seek feedback from trusted colleagues, friends, or family members. They can often provide insights into your abilities and limitations.

- **Monitor Your Well-being**: Regularly check in with yourself regarding your mental and physical health. If you notice a consistent negative impact, it might indicate you're reaching your limits.

- **Time Management**: Assess your time management skills. Are you consistently able to complete tasks within set timeframes, or do you find yourself constantly running out of time?

- **Experiment and Adjust**: Experiment with different levels of workload or responsibility and adjust based on your comfort and ability to manage effectively.

- **Professional Assessment**: In some cases, it may be helpful to seek a professional assessment, especially for tasks requiring specific skills or expertise.

- **Consider External Factors**: External factors like family responsibilities, financial resources, and support systems play a significant role in determining what you can achieve. Assess these factors realistically.

- **Embrace Flexibility**: Be open to adjusting your perception of your limits. Flexibility allows you to adapt to changing circumstances and opportunities for growth.

By understanding and respecting your limits, you can set yourself up for success and well-being, avoiding the pitfalls of overcommitment and burnout. Remember, limits can change over time with experience, personal growth, and changes in circumstances, so periodic reassessment is beneficial.

Technology

In 2020, 53% of caregivers had used some form of technology or software for caregiving tasks (AARP 2020), which is quite low, if you ask me! As intimidating as some technology is, leveraging technology can significantly enhance the caregiving experience by making tasks more manageable, improving communication, and providing entertainment and comfort to the care recipient. Use apps and tools to help organize caregiving tasks and manage time effectively. Here are various ways caregivers can use technology to facilitate caregiving:

- **Shared Workspace with Co-caregivers**: Create and share cloud-based documents or spreadsheets to help manage care duties.

- **Health Monitoring Apps**: Use apps to track the care recipient's medical appointments, medication schedules, and health parameters like blood pressure or blood sugar levels. Apps like CareZone or Medisafe can help manage these aspects efficiently.

- **Communication Tools**: Utilize video calling platforms like Skype, Zoom, or FaceTime to stay in touch with family members, especially if they live far away. This helps in coordinating care and keeping everyone updated.

- **Medication Dispensers and Reminders**: Automated medication dispensers and reminder apps can ensure that medications are taken correctly and on time, reducing the risk of missed doses.

- **Wearable Health Devices**: Wearable devices like smartwatches can monitor vital signs, track physical activity, and even alert caregivers in case of falls or unusual activities.

- **Online Grocery and Medicine Delivery**: Leverage online delivery services for groceries, medications, and other essentials. This is particularly useful for caregivers with time constraints.

- **Home Safety and Monitoring Systems**: Install home monitoring systems with sensors or cameras to ensure the safety of the care recipient, especially for those with dementia or mobility issues.

- **Entertainment and Mental Stimulation**: Tablets or smart devices can be used to access entertainment like music, audiobooks, or games, which are great for mental stimulation and relaxation.

- **Telemedicine Services**: Use telemedicine platforms for virtual doctor's appointments, which can be more convenient than in-person visits, especially for routine check-ups.

- **Online Support Groups and Resources**: Participate in online caregiver support groups and forums for advice, emotional support, and caregiving tips.

- **Digital Calendars and Scheduling Tools**: Utilize digital calendars and scheduling tools to organize and share caregiving duties among family members.

- **Mobile Safety Apps**: Apps like Life360 or medical alert systems can provide peace of mind by sending alerts or tracking the location of the care recipient.

- **Educational Resources**: Access online courses, webinars, and articles to stay informed about the care recipient's condition and the latest caregiving strategies.

- **Smart Home Devices**: Implement smart home technology like voice-activated systems, automated lighting, and thermostats to simplify household management.

- **Relaxation and Exercise Apps**: Encourage the use of relaxation and exercise apps to promote physical and mental well-being for both the caregiver and the care recipient.

By integrating these technological tools into the caregiving routine, caregivers can enhance the quality of care, improve communication, and find more time for personal care and enjoyment.

Closing

As we reach the conclusion of this guide, it's essential to reflect on the multifaceted journey of caregiving, a path filled with challenges, learning, and the potential for personal growth. Throughout this book, we've explored the diverse conditions and dynamics that shape the caregiving experience, from managing mental health conditions and navigating complex family roles to understanding the impact of historic family influences. Each chapter has provided insights into the unique challenges these factors present, offering practical advice and emotional support to help you manage this demanding yet rewarding role.

Caregiving is not a one-size-fits-all role; it's a deeply personal experience influenced by numerous factors. Whether dealing with mental health conditions like depression, OCD, or addiction, or navigating family dynamics as the Responsible Child, Peacekeeper, or even the Overlooked One, caregivers face a myriad of emotional and practical challenges. The historic influences of your family, including past traumas and healthcare beliefs, further add layers of complexity to the caregiving role.

In the face of the struggles and uncertainties of caregiving, it's crucial to remember the strength and resilience you've already shown. Each day you provide care, you're making a significant difference in the life of your loved one. This journey, as challenging as it may be, is also an opportunity for incredible personal growth and deepening of family bonds.

As a caregiver, you are more than just the sum of your duties. You are a whole human with needs, dreams, and aspirations. Balancing caregiving with personal growth and fulfillment is not just beneficial but essential. It's this balance that will sustain you through the challenges, enable you to provide the best care possible, and lead a fulfilling life.

As we close here, remember that caregiving is a journey of love, patience, and resilience. It's a role that may test your limits but also reveals your capacity for compassion and strength. Keep moving forward with determination, armed with the knowledge, strategies, and support you've gained, and always remember to care for the many facets within you.

Acknowledgements

This book would not have been possible without the support and contributions of some truly lovely people.

Tomás, thank you for your many brainstorming sessions and unwavering encouragement—even while challenging me to rethink my approach. Alina, your comic relief has brightened even the longest writing days and reminded me to take time to laugh.

Mom, I am endlessly grateful for your linguistic expertise and thoughtful feedback, which elevated this work in ways only you could.

Dad, you inspired many of the ideas here, and keep me always looking on the bright side of life.

Mercedes, your honest reviews of countless iterations of this book have been invaluable—thank you for your patience and sharp eye.

And to my amazing editor, Lisa, your thoroughness and positivity have been a gift to this process. Your insights ensured that this book became the best version of itself.

From the bottom of my heart, thank you all.

About the Author

Dr. Alexis Olson specializes in neuropsychological evaluation and therapy with individuals and their loved ones affected by brain injury, neurodegenerative disease, and chronic pain and illness. She naturally transitioned to supporting caregivers when many of her patients required the assistance of loved ones whose needs became apparent yet little psychological support was in sight for those informal caregivers. She has worked with caregivers of individuals with a range of conditions, from lifelong spinal cord injury to Parkinson's disease. Her background includes a Ph.D. in Clinical Psychology from the University of California, Santa Barbara. Find out more about Dr. Alexis Olson at www.doctorolson.com.

Works Cited

Algoe, S. B., Gable, S. L., & Maisel, N. C. (2010). It's the little things: Everyday gratitude as a booster shot for romantic relationships. Personal relationships, 17(2), 217-233.

Applebaum, A. J., Buda, K. L., Schofield, E., Farberov, M., Teitelbaum, N. D., Evans, K., ... & Cannady, R. S. (2018). Exploring the cancer caregiver's journey through web-based Meaning-Centered Psychotherapy. Psycho-oncology, 27(3), 847-856.

Applebaum, A. J., Baser, R. E., Roberts, K. E., Lynch, K., Gebert, R., Breitbart, W. S., & Diamond, E. L. (2022). Meaning-Centered Psychotherapy for Cancer Caregivers: A pilot trial among caregivers of patients with glioblastoma multiforme. Translational Behavioral Medicine, 12(8), 841-852.

Applebaum, A. J. B. (2024). Meaning-Centered Psychotherapy for Cancer Caregivers: Therapist Manual and Caregiver Workbook. Oxford University Press.

Archangels. (n.d.). Insights. Retrieved June 8, 2024, from https://www.archangels.me/insights

Baharudin, A. D., Din, N. C., Subramaniam, P., & Razali, R. (2019). The associations between behavioral-psychological symptoms of dementia (BPSD) and coping strategy, burden of care and personality style among low-income caregivers of patients with dementia. BMC public health, 19, 1-12.

Boreham, I. D., & Schutte, N. S. (2023). The relationship between purpose in life and depression and anxiety: A meta-analysis. Journal of clinical psychology, 79(12), 2736-2767.

Centers for Disease Control and Prevention. (2024). Public health strategy for supporting family caregivers. U.S. Department of Health and Human Services.

Ecker, Y., Busch, A. W., Schreiber, S., & Imhoff, R. (2023). From social traditions to personalized routines: Maintenance goals as a resilience factor. European Journal of Social Psychology.

Kurinobu, T., Tomita, A., & Matsukuma, R. (2024). Effects of family caregivers keeping a "Good Things Diary of Caregiving" on mental health, caregiving burden, and positive evaluations of caregiving: A randomized controlled trial. Journal of Affective Disorders Reports, 17, 100830.

Hajek, A., & König, H. H. (2018). The relation between personality, informal caregiving, life satisfaction and health-related quality of life: evidence of a longitudinal study. Quality of Life Research, 27, 1249-1256.

Kim, S., Park, Y., & Headrick, L. (2018). Daily micro-breaks and job performance: General work engagement as a cross-level moderator. Journal of Applied Psychology, 103(7), 772.

Kranabetter, C., & Niessen, C. (2019). Appreciation and depressive symptoms: The moderating role of need satisfaction. Journal of occupational health psychology, 24(6), 629.

Lambert, N. M., Fincham, F. D., & Stillman, T. F. (2012). Gratitude and depressive symptoms: The role of positive reframing and positive emotion. Cognition & emotion, 26(4), 615-633.

Luchetti, M., Terracciano, A., Stephan, Y., Aschwanden, D., & Sutin, A. R. (2021). Personality and psychological health in caregivers of older relatives: A case-control study. Aging & mental health, 25(9), 1692-1700.

Manzini CSS, do Vale FAC. Emotional disorders evidenced by family caregivers of older people with Alzheimer's disease. Dement Neuropsychol. 2020 Jan-Mar;14(1):56-61. doi: 10.1590/1980-57642020dn14-010009. PMID: 32206199; PMCID: PMC7077868.

Melo, G., Maroco, J., Lima-Basto, M., & de Mendonça, A. (2017). Personality of the caregiver influences the use of strategies to deal with the behavior of persons with dementia. Geriatric nursing, 38(1), 63-69.

Miller, L., Wickramaratne, P., Hao, X., McClintock, C. H., Pan, L., Svob, C., & Weissman, M. M. (2021). Altruism and "love of neighbor" offer neuroanatomical protection against depression. Psychiatry Research: Neuroimaging, 315, 111326.

Pereira-Morales, A. J., Adan, A., & Forero, D. A. (2019). Perceived stress as a mediator of the relationship between neuroticism and depression and anxiety symptoms. Current Psychology, 38, 66-74.

Substance Abuse and Mental Health Services Administration. (2023). 2021 National Survey on Drug Use and Health: Detailed tables (HHS Publication No. PEP22-07-01-001). U.S. Department of Health and Human Services.

Sievertsen, H. H., Gino, F., & Piovesan, M. (2016). Cognitive fatigue influences students' performance on standardized tests. Proceedings of the National Academy of Sciences, 113(10), 2621-2624.

Vinograd, M., Williams, A., Sun, M., Bobova, L., Wolitzky-Taylor, K. B., Vrshek-Schallhorn, S., ... & Craske, M. G. (2020). Neuroticism and interpretive bias as risk factors for anxiety and depression. Clinical Psychological Science, 8(4), 641-656.

Witvliet, C. V., Richie, F. J., Root Luna, L. M., & Van Tongeren, D. R. (2019). Gratitude predicts hope and happiness: A two-study assessment of traits and states. The Journal of Positive Psychology, 14(3), 271-282.

Zhao, S., Du, H., Li, Q., Wu, Q., & Chi, P. (2021). Growth mindset of socioeconomic status boosts subjective well-being: A longitudinal study. Personality and Individual Differences, 168, 110301.